W9-BPM-693

The
Power in Your
Money
Personality

8 Ways to Balance
Your Urge to Splurge
With Your Craving for Saving

Susan Zimmerman, LMFT, ChFC

Beaver's Pond Press, Inc.

The Power in Your Money Personality: 8 Ways to Balance Your Urge to Splurge With Your Craving for Saving

The fiscal rascals™, money rascals™, Aryhmatherapy™, COOL/FOOL Rule™, AHA™, AIM™, BOB™ ,PAT™, PETS™, Asher™, Basher™, Casher™, Clasher™, Dasher™, Flasher™, Rasher™, Stasher™ are claimed as trademarks of ZFG.

ISBN:193164618X
LCC:20011095587

Publisher: Beaver's Pond Press

Beaver's Pond Press, Inc.

Editor: Bill Perron
Illustrator: Caroline Wolf
Cover Design: Dunn+Associates
Photographer: Rod Oman, The Imagery
Printed in the United States of America

01 01 03   1 2 3 4 5

Contents

Acknowledgments

Ideas are created from such a vast number of life experiences and people encounters, it is difficult to do justice to them all. I would like to thank my family, clients and colleagues who gave me enthusiastic feedback and encouragement throughout my work on this subject.

To my husband and business partner, Steve, your support made this book possible. To Katie, Jamison, Sari and Desiree, thanks for showing us that the money lessons we have force-fed you from the time you earned your first nickels have served you well.

To the special interest group on the psychology of money of the Financial Planning Association in Minneapolis, thank you. A fond thank you is extended to Kathi Dunn for her book cover graphics design and to Susan Kendrick for her cover writing. A special thanks to Caroline Wolf (at right), who enthusiastically illustrated each money rascal with her wonderful, creative flair.

My deepest gratitude is extended to the Alfred Adler Graduate School faculty and associates for your academic excellence and encouragement during my thesis, "Using Individual Psychology as Therapeutic Intervention in American Money Management and Savings Problems." Thank you to my LMFT associates and supervisors for sharing your professional experience and wisdom: Mim Pew, Ginny D'Angelo, Brier Miller, Steven Erickson, and Susan Pye Brokaw. The learning never stops!

And finally, thanks, Dad. Thank you for your strength and courage throughout your battle with cancer. We swam together in an "ocean of emotion" in your last days and I will never forget the power of that special journey we traveled. The lessons and the joy of the tears we cried together do live on.

BACKGROUND

Many people who seek credit, budget or financial counseling follow recommended practices only long enough to relieve a specific immediate problem, often tied to a financial crisis point such as credit card debt. Short term relief, however, doesn't solve the real problem and the original behavior often resumes, bringing the problem back. When this becomes the pattern, often the recurring problem has grown larger and more difficult to solve.

Researchers are finding that there is also a health price paid due to financial anxiety, ranging from heart attacks and insomnia to explosive emotions and extreme fatigue. When financial needs are neglected or avoided, people are vulnerable to the countless ways problems can worsen, sometimes with the mere passage of time. At older ages, for example, health care alone can strain their ability to pay for needed services.

If, instead, individuals could discover the underlying reasons for the behavior, the likelihood of lasting long term solutions is increased. The money rascal personalities introduce the concept of "fiscal therapy" to help reveal unconscious mistaken beliefs about money and how that is linked to emotional and behavioral reactions to it. This is a critical component to financial well-being, especially when operating in a society that encourages instant gratification through mass spending, debt and consumerism.

In countless studies of household spending and assets, retirement plan participation, net worth, credit card debt and bankruptcies, it appears that many Americans are experiencing tremendous financial difficulties. Personal bankruptcies nearly doubled in the '90s, to 1.2 million a year. They have nearly quadrupled in the last 20 years.

Marketing strategists know how to appeal to impulse buying, which seems to deliberately encourage excessive consumerism.

The Power in Your Money Personality

The credit card industry has become more aggressive in their solicitations, sending 3 billion pieces of mail annually (compared to 900 million sent out in 1992). Today, the average credit card balance per household is $7,500 (compared to $3,000 in 1990). Debt is rising faster than salaries. According to a March 2000 Federal Reserve Statistical Release, the total outstanding consumer credit for the first quarter of 2000 was $132 billion. Credit cards issued in 2001 number 1.5 billion, with $560 billion in outstanding credit card debt in the United States.

The percentage of people who are more than 60 days late on their credit payments is up by more than a third from 1992 to 1998 for 35- to 44-year-olds, and for 45- to 54-year-olds, late payments are up by almost two-thirds. The proportion of this debt belonging to young people in their teens and early 20s is increasing. A survey of recent college graduates found that 35 percent had debt payments of more than $1000 a month, unrelated to their educational costs.

Spending is up and savings are down. In 1990 the typical US household saved 7.8 percent of its income. Last year that same family spent .1 percent more than it earned. The "urge to splurge" is certainly alive and well in the United States. When it comes to spending in the U.S., it appears the motto should be *"America - Land of the free spenders and home of the brave debtors!"*

Many factors contribute to, or trigger behaviors that become almost addictive or compulsive. Indeed, our society does seem to reinforce multiple addictive behaviors. Many such behaviors are directly related to money matters, such as workaholism and overspending. It is as though we get hooked on the compulsive styles of working, shopping and the use of credit cards to purchase items that provide short-lived, if any, genuine

> ...it appears the motto should be "America - Land of the free spenders and home of the brave debtors!"

gratification. One overall cultural expectation seems to be that money is, or somehow *should be,* directly responsible for individuals' feelings of mental well being.

Often what lies beneath compulsive behaviors, in general, is a feeling of personal inadequacy and low self-esteem. Compulsive uses of money become a type of "self-medicating" to fill the void and feel better. The problem with this as a coping behavior is that it provides only temporary relief.

These factors explain in part, why, statistically, most purchases are not for replacement of worn out items. It also provides clues as to why Americans continue to report a lack of satisfaction from their spending behaviors. Just as overeating junk food has been called consuming "empty calories," spending money on unnecessary or unaffordable material goods can be called "empty buying." Neither behavior feeds a healthy or satisfying long-term result, and both seem to trigger more of the same problematic habits. With this lack of contentment coupled with high stress that damages health, one might expect that the pursuit of more money and/or more spending itself would stop, but instead it is growing.

In today's financial world, there are more options and choices for individual financial management than ever before. The need for retirement planning and personal savings is also greater than before, due to many factors. The number of years people live in retirement has dramatically increased, yet the contribution that Social Security provides is minimal. The decrease in employer-managed retirement savings plans places a greater responsibility for retirement income on employee contributions such as 401K plans. Feeling unprepared for this responsibility, it can overwhelm and discourage even the ultra-analytical types.

Money issues can house unconscious expectations and meanings that cause us to lose sight of what exactly we *are* in pursuit of. Is it love? Security? Prestige? Freedom? Comfort? Success? By what yardstick are we measuring it? Have we lost sight of our own intrinsic human value by focusing on money exclusively?

The Power in Your Money Personality

The psychological component of money behavior is typically not addressed by financial planners or debt counselors. That is why *The Power in Your Money Personality* was written. I invite you to accompany the eight money rascal personality types as they romp their way through a pursuit of *psychological self awareness about money and financial behavior,* instead of the pursuit of money itself or the things it can buy.

The money rascals can lead us to an understanding of our unique "urge to splurge or craving for saving." They can free our spirits from the bondage of "shopaholism" or the empty striving for social status. They help reveal our motivations and styles while showing us a new path to fiscal fitness. When money habits are courageously adjusted from the *inside out* and put into balance, financial freedom lasts a lifetime, passing on wisdom through countless generations.

The Power in Your Money Personality

I have a great money personality,
Full of ingredients like a recipe.
But if I get too much of a good thing,
The taste is bitter and gives me a sting!
I wonder if my dollars would approve,
Of all the ways I try to make them groove?

How does your money personality have power?

It has the power to steer your decisions and behaviors with money. It has the power to generate painful or joyful emotions related to money. And it has the power to fool you into believing something that is not true *for you.*

What *is* your money personality?

We all have a unique blend of Physical, Emotional, Thought, and Social (PETS) habits with money, like a secret recipe. Those PETS are the ingredients of your money personality. Think of the acronym 'PET' to simply mean favorite or indulged (remember who the teacher's pet was in school?). Think of your money personality as all your favorite ways of thinking, feeling and handling your money.

Where does your money personality come from?

Money "personality" develops from a combination of sociological and experiential factors. The habits and patterns we acquire with money are the result of our deeply personal interpretations of the models we have been exposed to along the way.

Sometimes we make "promises" to ourselves that become conscious or unconscious goals about our financial life. These promises accumulate, forming our unique Bundle Of Beliefs (BOB) about money. Our special blend of beliefs has tremendous influence on our financial behavior. The only problem with such an influence is that many of the beliefs misdirect us in our financial life, because they stem from inaccurate conclusions we have drawn from earlier life events.

Can your money personality change?

YES! That's what this book is about. We can change our habitual behaviors and our psychological patterns with money. Start by discovering what your dominant styles with money have been. Some tend to be driven by that powerful "urge to splurge." Others "crave to save." There are eight money personality types identified in the chapters ahead. They represent the eight ways to balance out the habits you have identified as problematic, whether you have too much of the traits, or not enough. Create greater balance to your mix of money personalities by first "borrowing" useful traits from the types you lack, practicing them, and finally owning them as you experience a new and improved financial life.

Meet and claim the 8 money rascals

The money or fiscal rascals, when out of balance or overly dominant in one's style, are known for making mischief in our financial lives. Actually, the money rascals can be our best friend or our worst mischievous trouble maker when it comes to money. They are a light-hearted group of eight types of money "personalities" that characterize spending and other financial styles. Before describing each type, let's look at some terms we'll be using.

fiscal - describes issues relating to finances and *money,* it is used interchangeably with money

rascal - mischievous traits and tendencies in our personalities that steer our behavior, such as an overly dominant "urge to splurge" or "craving for saving."

fiscal rascals - represent the troublesome financial characteristics that may "visit" our psyches and have an unbalancing effect on our money behaviors, especially during times of stress.

money rascals - the same as fiscal rascal, though they represent a more tamed, or rebalanced mix of rascals after making desired changes.

personality - all the *physical, emotional, thought, and social* (PETS) characteristics of an individual.

These definitions will be used as a framework for assessing and working with the financial aspect of personality. Our money behaviors - namely spending, organizing, saving, thinking and emotional habits often mystify us. We may experience strong emotional reactions to money matters and wonder where the intensity came from. The money rascals can help us solve this personal mystery and begin to understand the psychological dynamics in our financial lives.

Is one rascal better than another?

Not at all. It is important to note here that each fiscal rascal type has potential advantages and disadvantages, yet none is superior to another. Some have pesky habits that are more difficult to change than others, especially if societal systems reinforce them. It is up to each individual to determine whether any of the style patterns in the rascals identified are creating problems in his or her life.

In some instances the problem could be a relational one, where one person is satisfied and content, while the other is frustrated and dissatisfied. Getting to know and understand these rascals and the extent to which they may be present in our personality styles is a critical aspect of resolving current conflicts. The awareness they encourage can also help prevent additional problems in the future.

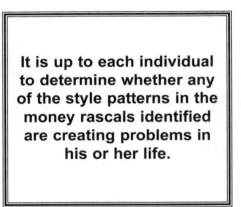

It is up to each individual to determine whether any of the style patterns in the money rascals identified are creating problems in his or her life.

What is Arhymatherapy?

You have probably heard of aromatherapy, which uses a variety of scents to produce postitive moods. Well, artistically placed rhyming words can do the same thing! Pronounced *a-rhyme'-a-therapy,* it is demonstrated throughout *The Power in Your Money Personality,* to lighten up the sometimes heavy topic of money and emotions. It adds rhythm and rhymes to the topic at hand, sometimes with a bit of playful teasing and exaggeration to create a healthy chuckle at ourselves.

Arhymatherapy is designed to help us see things we might otherwise miss (perhaps because we're too serious or stressed out), and feel an uplifted and positive mood. When we feel good, we can tackle change and create new habits that improve our well being.

The rhyming, light-hearted names of the money rascals were created to help minimize any preconceived judgments about what traits each type might have. It is important to stay as unbiased as possible when examining money attitudes, as there are no absolutes. What seems genuinely right to one person may contradict deeply held values of another. As you read the upcoming sections for each rascal, you may recognize yourself in several. It is quite common for us to display the qualities of different rascals at different times.

The assessment questionnaire

Now, go to the fiscal rascal questionnaire found in the Appendix to assess, or claim your money personalities. It is best to complete the fiscal rascal questionnaire **before** you study the descriptions. That way you won't be tempted to answer the questions in a biased way. Although no rascal is right or wrong, good or bad, superior or inferior, you may naturally favor one over another once you read about them. This can affect how you respond to the questions.

Answer each item of the questionnaire. You may feel that none of the answers reflect how you would respond. In that case, choose the response that *most closely* fits how you would think, act, or feel in the situation given. If you find more than one answer that feels absolutely equal in your reaction, circle both and count them in your score. The rascals do sometimes change from one life period to another. Don't choose responses based on how you would *like* to be, but how you *actually are* at this stage of your life.

Then record your scores on the answer sheet and plot your rascals on the charts.

Staking Your Claim

Now that you have scored your questionnaire, are you ready to **"claim"** your rascals? For the purpose of this exercise, "claim" simply means *accepting that these rascals exist to some extent in your financial style.*

You may find that two or three rascal styles emerge as dominant, rather than just one. That's fine. In fact, having relatively even scores on all the rascals across the continuum may indicate a healthy balance. Scores in any one rascal of five or higher, may signify occasionally getting "too much of a good thing."

With scores of seven or higher in any rascal, you may be experiencing the phenomenon of "too much of a good thing too often!" The highest score you can get for any one rascal is ten (unless you selected more than one choice in some of the questions).

A point worthy of note here, is that our American culture is such a spending-oriented one, that to achieve a healthy spending/saving balance, the saving scores need to outweigh the spending ones. Otherwise, the societal pressure to spend may dominate our choices, usually resulting in financial shortages unless a plan is put in place.

Regardless of your scores, it is useful to ask yourself if any of the traits of the money rascals have caused problems in your financial life or relationships.

Where are you on the continuum?

URGE TO SPLURGE							CRAVE TO SAVE
◄────────────							──────────────►
Flasher	Rasher	Clasher	Dasher	Basher	Asher	Casher	Stasher
prestige spender	impulsive shopper	conflicting desires	busy avoider	money is bad	fearful worries	safe saver hates debt	growth investor

Are you more on the saver end or the spender end? Do you have one dominant money personality, or more? Which rascal (or rascals) scored the highest?

The first two rascals on the left end of the continuum are both spenders (the urge to splurge) - they vary primarily in their purchase preferences and impulsivity. The opposite end shows two different types of saving rascals (crave to save). We'll get into more detail on the personality types in later chapters.

From a financial planning perspective, if you have been neglecting to save and invest, your rebalancing goal may be to begin working more toward the crave-to-save end of the continuum. This would help you create greater comfort and less financial stress later in life.

One way to reframe this, is to think in terms of **enjoying today and tomorrow equally.** If you spend all of your earnings today, you have little chance of having the freedom to spend even modestly in the future. From a present day perspective, the objective is to "tame" some of the problematic money habits that either keep you stressed or behind where you want to be financially.

Howdy pardner. What's your score?

If you and a spouse or partner are both doing the assessment, you can record both scores on the continuum. Put one above and one below the line. Circle your top two or three scores and compare how you are alike and different. You can also go back to the questionnaire and use it as a discussion tool for sharing more information about your reactions to the questions. If you came up with a response not listed in the question, share it with your partner.

Were either of you surprised? As a partnership, are you clashing? How do you handle conflicts or indecision about money? Do you talk? yell? lie? avoid? sneak? overpower? intimidate? give in? give up? postpone? flee? compromise? take turns winning? How do you feel about these techniques? What would you like to improve?

Couples often become masterfully creative in avoiding or dealing with money conflict. Unfortunately, sometimes all they have actually accomplished is to fan the flame of problems, paving the way for a bigger inferno blast later! Ironically, the very thing that was part of the attraction in courtship often turns into the source of irrtation and clashing when money is merged. Patterns emerge and repeat themselves, often in unhealthy ways. (See the chapter on conflict resolution for more information about the fiscal rascals in relationships.)

Let's briefly meet the Money Rascals now

The money rascals each have a unique set of personality traits and beliefs about money. One of the concepts that will be developed in each is that of unconscious beliefs. These are often what is driving the mischievous part of the rascals' actions. It helps explain why we act the way we do with money. Each rascal has a chapter that details their most common Physical, Emotional, Thinking, and Social habits, but for now, here is a brief look at their characteristics.

Casher and **Stasher** are the rascals who like to save. They seem to have a natural craving for saving. Casher is the debt-hating, safe, secure *cash* savings seeker, who likes to organize and track money. Stasher is the investor looking to accumulate wealth by *stashing* money away for higher returns.

Flasher and **Rasher** have the urge to splurge. The primary difference between them is what they "get" from their splurging. Flasher is seeking prestige, status or image, which usually translates into large, *flashy* expenditures. Rasher, on the other hand, frequently makes *rash* and impulsive decisions with fiscal matters. Rasher likes the shopping experience itself - the search, the selection, the transaction and the many sensations of making a purchase.

Asher was named because s/he can become ashen and pale over money worries, insecurity, or anxiety. Regardless of how much money Asher has, fear of loss or losing control is dominant. Asher craves security, yet has difficulty finding it.

Basher *bashes* wealth, harshly criticizing it. Basher believes it spoils the goodness of people. Basher lives ultra-modestly to demonstrate virtue and purity of values. Basher craves virtue.

Dasher, like Santa's reindeer, is fast. As you might guess by the name, Dasher is the rascal who is busy *dashing* from one activity to another - all except money activities, that is.

Clasher is the undecided rascal. Clasher is ambivalent, with conflicting desires that *clash* with each other, causing ever-changing behavior and actions that may appear to be direct opposites. Clasher's urge is to settle ambivalent feelings.

The Rascals	The Delightful Side	The Frightful Side
Flasher	Fun, entertaining, meal ticket, treater, loans money, spontaneous, lives for today, giving, decisive, generous, has flair	Braggart, show off, bossy, puts others down, planless, debt-ridden, domineering, no savings, impulsive, compulsive, stubborn, overspends, overborrows, overlends
Rasher	Lives for today, giving, light-hearted, creative, interesting, diverse, people-pleasing, spontaneous, fun loving, pleasure seeker/finder	No savings, impulsive, expects like behavior in return, debt-ridden, unorganized, compulsive, unreliable, self-centered, self-indulgent, neglects/ignores future
Dasher	Action-packed, diverse experience, interesting, creative, social, outgoing, efficient	Uptight, late, avoids conflict, neglects planning, under-organized, procrastinates, distracted
Clasher	Sincere, good intentions, adaptable, sometimes energized, open-minded, curious	Insecure, defensive, indecisive, confused, easily swayed, frustrated, frustrating, changes too often
Basher	Integrity, ethical, charitable, helpful, conviction, committed, thoughtful, non-materialistic, virtuous	Dull, no fun, stubborn, bland, unchanging, selfless, judgmental, bitter, imposes values, under-spends
Asher	Responsive, helpful, pensive, careful, needs to feel needed, pragmatic, frugal, proactive	Depressed, uptight and tight, crabby, too serious, over cautious, self-punishing, distracted, a drag
Casher	Dependable, reliable, accurate, organized, accessible savings, disciplined, thrifty	Compulsive planner, won't lend a dime, tightwad, over-analytical, rigid, perfectionistic, too cautious
Stasher	Optimistic, money stashed for investment growth, may loan money, planful, tolerates fluctuation	Under-spends, compulsive trading, investment risk too high, addicted to excitement, pushy, unrealistic

Using the book as a guide

I would encourage you to finish this chapter for Pat and Kay's case examples. Look over the "Delightful/Frightful" chart for a glimpse of the strengths and weaknesses of the rascal personality traits. Who knows who you might recognize there!

Then review the next section, **Taming Your Fiscal Rascals,** before going to each rascal chapter. Both define important terminology and concepts that appear in all of the rascal case studies. They are a key component of helping you make the most of the guidelines and strategies for change provided with each rascal.

Then go to the individual fiscal rascal chapters in any order you prefer. Out of curiosity, most people look up their dominant rascals first.

You will find helpful tips with all of the rascal chapters, whether your score reflects the presence of a rascal in your money personality or not. So, regardless of what order you read them in, do visit them all. Maybe they'll also help you understand someone *else* in your life!

Remember, the goal is to achieve greater *balance* in your urge to splurge and your craving for saving.

Habits of thought

Most often, the behavioral patterns we fall into with money are the result of our own interpretations of the models we have been exposed to along the way. Not surprisingly, many of these interpretations were made in childhood and became little "invisible vows" we made to ourselves without even realizing it.

These vows, though unconscious, often have tremendous influence. That influence may steer our direction with greater power than the financial goals we consciously *think* we are in pursuit of. If the unconscious vows are in conflict with the conscious goals - guess which ones grab the steering wheel and move us *their* way? If you guessed the unconscious ones, you guessed right!

Think of an iceberg

One way to conceptualize our belief systems is to picture an iceberg. An awesome structure of ice broken off from a glacier and floating in the sea, much of its mass (about 85%) is beneath the surface of the water.

Unconscious thought is like the mass of ice under the water. Most of the time we cannot see that portion, and are unaware of its influence on the iceberg as a whole. But its influence is powerful and it moves the mass of ice.

Conscious thought is like the part of the iceberg we can see above the surface. We are aware of it because it is in plain view. Provided we are paying attention, we can maneuver around it to avoid damage from its jagged edges.

But the portion of ice below the water is vast and hidden from view. It takes special equipment and exploration to see it. If we remain unaware of it when it matters the most we may steer ourselves in a direction that causes damage (remember the Titanic). It would have been better to prevent the damage in the first place.

In making our way through life, becoming aware of what lies beneath the surface of our conscious thought can help us move in a positive direction. It can protect us from the "jagged edges" of poor choices that sabotage our genuine goals.

The money rascals can serve as that special equipment to look beneath the surface and explore what is normally unseen about our financial selves. That way we can steer our financial lives in the direction we truly want to go.

Let's look at an example to see what can happen when conscious goals oppose unconscious ones.

Pat's story

Pat grew up in a family whose earnings were modest. It was a struggle to make ends meet. They valued honesty, hard work, and caring. Their spending was quite disciplined and there were many things they had to do without. Much of their clothing came from thrift and discount stores and hand-me-downs. Pat felt sorry for his dad having to borrow the neighbor's chain saw, for example, rather than being able to own one.

Pat decided early on that when he grew up he would make a substantial income so that he wouldn't have to deny himself the nicer things money could buy. This was one of his conscious goals.

Pat, however, also recalled several occasions when his mother made disapproving comments about people who appeared to have high incomes and wealthier lifestyles. Her comments included remarks such as the ones in the next section.

Pat heard his mother's comments:

> *"Mrs. Brown is such a snob, she turns her nose up at anyone not in her precious women's club! I'm glad we're just 'good, honest folk.'"*

> *"All they care about is their money."*

> *"Look at them showing off their new car. That's disgusting."*

Pat, as a child, translated his mother's comments into several invisible, or unconscious beliefs that did not harmonize with his adult conscious income goal. These unconscious beliefs always had some conclusions attached to them. These "Pat" conclusions would steer his behavior so as not to contradict the deep-seated belief.

A child's conclusions, however, contain significant generalizations and other extremes. Pat was no exception and this process occurred, creating invisible beliefs and interpretations that conflicted with his conscious adult goals.

Unconscious conclusions hidden in Pat's mind:

Rich people are **always** snobs,
so if I am rich, it will make me a snob
(and that's bad so I better make sure that doesn't happen).

Rich people are disgusting and **unlovable**,
so if I am rich, I will be unlovable
(that would be unbearable, so I should prevent it).

You can't be both rich and be honest,
so if I am rich, I'll end up being **dishonest**
(I value honesty, so I'll choose it instead of wealth).

Rich people are unloving and uncaring,
so if I am rich, I will become **loveless**
(love is more important than wealth, so I'll avoid wealth).

Rich people are **nothing but** showoffs,
showoffs deserve to be rejected
(so if I am rich, I will be empty and rejected).

Pat appreciated his family values of honesty and decency, and he wanted to be a virtuous and giving person. He wanted to feel love and acceptance in his life.

Pat gets a job

Pat went to work in sales for a large pharmaceutical company. At first, he aggressively pursued his sales goals and his income was growing impressively. He was acting on his conscious goal to make a large income. After just a few months, Pat had already earned more than his father's annual income.

Pat started to feel wealthy and successful. For the next few months he slacked off, spending more and more time doing paper work and research activities. His income began to plummet. Though on a conscious level he told himself he was still working hard, that wasn't the case and the income from sales results had slowed to almost nothing.

13

What was going on with Pat?

While he did feel successful pursuing his income goals (his conscious goals), beneath these goals were Pat's unconscious conclusions as listed earlier. The two sets were in conflict with each other. Although the unconscious ones were invisible to Pat, they went to work on him. When he succeeded in producing his conscious income goals, his unconscious goals served him up a generous helping of guilt feelings.

He felt disloyal and almost ashamed of his money. Pat unconsciously feared that he would lose his values of love, honesty and caring for people if he became wealthier than "normal" (what he had become accustomed to growing up).

The respect he felt for his father made him uneasy earning so much more, especially given his invisible beliefs that rich people were disgusting, unlovable, dishonest snobs. Pat did not want to be rejected for his wealth, so his behavior began to assure that he would not achieve it. None of this was in Pat's awareness until he started uncovering his invisible beliefs and conclusions and seeing how perfectly they matched his income-sabotaging behaviors. His invisible beliefs were competing with the others, and they were winning! Can you see how this exemplifies Pat getting slashed by part of the iceberg beneath the surface?

Pat's money personality characteristics (PETS)

The **Physical** characteristics address our habits of handling and organizing our money. Do we spend it as soon as we get it? Do we put it in a piggy bank? Buy more high tech stock? Are we even aware of how much we have?

> *PHYSICAL: In Pat's case, he was relatively organized and disciplined about his use of money. He paid his bills on time and rarely used credit cards.*

The **Emotional** characteristics are how we *feel* about money. Are we anxious or apathetic? Proud or embarrassed? Depressed or excited? Confident or overwhelmed?

EMOTIONAL: Pat consciously felt proud and happy about his large income. Yet uneasiness and guilt feelings also existed (tied to his unconscious thoughts), along with a fear of the disapproval of others.

The **Thought** characteristics are how we think about money - both consciously and unconsciously.

THOUGHT: Pat consciously wanted to earn a large income. However, his unconscious thoughts, though distorted, told him that to do so would create severe consequences. He feared rejection, lovelessness, dishonesty and maybe even the loss of respect and loyalty of his family.

The **Social** characteristics of our money styles are about our external displays of money-related matters. What is our money behavior when we're around others? Is it consistent with how we behave when we're alone? Has it caused problems for us?

SOCIAL: Pat tended to be more reluctant to spend when around others than when alone. He was careful not to "show off" his money or the things it bought (honoring his mother's values).

Pat's dominant money personalities were Basher and Casher.

How does one change individual money habits?

The process of change begins with becoming aware of what invisible vows or beliefs are lurking beneath the surface of the conscious ones. This can be seen as a threat or as a great adventure. The fiscal rascals were created for, and will be of greatest service to those with an adventuresome spirit. The goal of the fiscal rascals is to refresh and enlighten, not scold and punish.

The money rascals have different tendencies, which when overly dominant, can lead to financial and other problems. Getting acquainted with them can help us get in touch with some of our own styles and understand a bit more clearly how we developed certain habits. Then, if we want to make changes we have some tools to help us with the task of creating a more balanced financial life.

Stepping into the cage and becoming a rascal-tamer

Once you have assessed and claimed the rascals dominating your financial style, the next step is to *tame* them. We tame our rascals by subduing and redirecting them. It's like a training program that takes them from their "savage" state and reprograms them for control. Each rascal in its "wild" state can cause problems in our financial serenity. It can be the reason for "wildly" overspending or "savagely" under spending. Or it can fan the flame of worry and anxiety. The purpose of taming, or subduing a fiscal rascal is to bring one's perceptions and behaviors about money into balance.

Kay tames her rascals - a case study

Kay grew up in an alcoholic household. Her father was known for his extravagant spending, especially when he was drinking. When out socially, he insisted on buying everyone's drinks and meals. He also bought only the **most expensive,** highest quality products, no matter what the purpose - clothing, cars, furniture, hardware. Kay always believed these purchases gave her dad a sense of prestige that he couldn't find within himself. These spending behaviors wreaked havoc with the family income, however, leaving a shortage for emergencies or other long term needs such as retirement.

Kay's mother tried to balance things out by buying only the **least expensive** items possible, shopping at thrift stores, clipping multiple grocery coupons and going to several stores to get the lowest prices.

Despite her parents' combined upper-middle class incomes, there were severe money shortages after Dad acted on his desires. As a result, Kay's family simply had to do without savings and other ordinary items. Kay vividly remembers her mother's anxiety each month as she "juggled" the bills, always having to choose a few that would not be paid until the next paycheck arrived.

When Kay grew up. . .

What then, became Kay's financial goals as an adult? Kay ended up with two sets of goals - her conscious/aware goals, and her unconscious/ unaware goals, which we have called her "invisible vows." Her conscious goals were the private promises she made to herself, resulting from experiences of financial stress in her years growing up.

The dominant theme of Kay's conscious goal was, "I will always be in **control** of my spending so that I don't have to live in fear of having too little money." Kay consciously wanted control, discipline, and security in her money life. What Kay was unaware of, however, were several invisible vows, or "guidance systems" that would steer her in a different direction - ones that conflicted with her conscious goals.

> **What Kay was unaware of, however, were several invisible vows, or "guidance systems" that would steer her in a different direction - ones that conflicted with her conscious goals.**

Kay's BOB (Bundle Of Beliefs)

This BOB (bundle of beliefs) created several "rules, measures and indicators" of what was *"normal"* for Kay. And when the two sets of rules didn't match, the result was a feeling of "BOBBING" around and being controlled by forces outside herself that she didn't understand (or even agree with). As we saw with Pat, it is often these mysterious forces that get their way in the end unless we become aware of them and make corrections.

Kay's BOB list included mistaken conclusions such as:

- *There is never enough money.*
- *I am only worthwhile if I show off my success with flashy items.*
- *Don't ever talk about money directly.*
- *Live only for today - the future doesn't matter.*

17

- *Saving never happens.*
- *Always buy the most expensive items.*
- *Always buy the least expensive items.*
- *The man always dominates the money decisions.*
- *Chaos and stress are normal.*
- *Money is something to fight about.*
- *Never ask for money.*

Notice that some of the BOB items contradict each other. It is this clashing that can cause emotional upheaval and a persistent sense of frustration or dissatisfaction. The beliefs also reveal an all-or-nothing, black-and-white thinking pattern. Such extremes in Kay's thinking originated as a child's conclusions about life, her place in it, and how to react to life's situations.

This is precisely the problem with the invisible BOB! These beliefs are created by a child's limited intellectual capacity to formulate useful interpretations of early life experience. They are then applied broadly in life events as they occur. Often the conclusions reached by the child apply the all-or-nothing interpretations in a misguided pattern. Words such as 'always,' 'never' and 'only if,' are part of the misguided belief system.

Kay as an adult

How did Kay's bundle of beliefs cause her to veer off course? Kay began her adult life with a good job and a decent income. She honored the conscious promise she had made to herself of financial stability, by setting up a savings account. She diligently put 15% of her income into it each month. Kay knew she never wanted to have the anxiety her mother experienced. Without the existence of this goal, she most likely would have spent her money instead of saving it.

The balance grew to an amount that gave Kay the security of knowing she would be okay for at least three months if she lost her job. Yet she felt funny, strange and almost bored! This was an unfamiliar feeling. Having such security actually felt *abnormal*. This was not in Kay's conscious awareness, but it was driving her inclination to give in to the powerful urge to splurge on the new stereo and big screen TV she had been looking at.

Kay was having more and more difficulty fighting that nagging feeling that she was depriving herself of the fun stuff that would make "today" happier and more exciting.

Remember, one of Kay's hidden beliefs was that the man makes the financial decisions. Although Kay was single, her father's style had been very influential to her. When Kay behaved in a way that opposed her father's style, she could only describe the feeling as "not normal." Buying the TV would feel normal.

Kay's fiscal rascal assessment

Kay's fiscal rascal assessment revealed one dominant personality type with three others tied for a close second place. The dominant one was **Clasher -** the rascal known for sabotaging efforts to save money because one goal or desire *clashes* with another.

Kay's conscious goals were most closely linked to her mother's style - craving for saving, being responsible with money, planning for the future, and having an organized way of meeting her obligations. This reflected the **Casher** style.

But Kay's subconscious goals had a voice, too. Linked to her father's *flashy* style of spending, she had invisible beliefs and urges to be irresponsible and lavish in her spending. This was the **Flasher** rascal. These two styles created the powerful and frustrating Clasher personality traits in Kay.

Kay's other fiscal rascal was **Asher,** reflecting her worry about money. Asher is the rascal who is insecure and anxious about money, and often accompanies Clasher because of the unpredictable opposing and conflicting styles of money handling.

Kay began taming her fiscal rascals by first acknowledging the existence of her underlying Bundle of Beliefs (BOB). This unmasked their sneaky "invisibility." Next, Kay reconstructed each misguided belief so that it fit her genuine beliefs. She looked at each previously hidden belief and made a conscious decision to agree or disagree with it. If she disagreed with it, she stated her rejection of it and then reconstructed it.

Kay changed her beliefs:

From. . .	To. . .
"There is never enough money."	"I have enough money to provide for my needs."
"I am only worthwhile if I show off my success with prestigious items."	"I am worthwhile regardless of my material possessions."

Additional Steps taken by Kay

- She added her existing *useful* financial goals to the list.

- Kay kept them visible in several places so that she could reaffirm the reconstructed beliefs several times each day.

- Kay changed each mistaken belief to fit her genuine beliefs, values and goals.

- She put copies in her checkbook, taped them to her bathroom mirror, in her calendar and on her refrigerator.

- Kay read the list out loud each morning and evening and when making financial decisions, she referred to the list to make sure she was guided by her true beliefs instead of the old, misdirected ones.

Kay's list of "FOOL Rules"

A second exercise Kay did after reviewing her beliefs, was to list the rules of behavior her beliefs had created. These forces had unknowingly served as a guidance system for her. She could then see how her own "rules" were a disservice to her and had caused her to get results in her financial life that didn't match her conscious, genuine goals.

Kay first listed her **F**amily **O**f **O**rigin **L**essons **(FOOL Rules)** that she had unknowingly *created for herself* from **mistaken conclusions** she had drawn from earlier life experience. Kay commented, "The rules are like a list of 'shoulds' carried around inside my head that tell me whether I'm okay or not!" And if they told her she was off the normal track and in unfamiliar territory, they FOOLED her. They would direct her to take actions that would return her to *"normal."*

Remember, however, that chaos and stress were Kay's unconscious definition of normal. Kay's fiscal rascals, therefore, steered her toward chaos to get her back into that old familiar territory. Not surprisingly, the FOOL Rules often appear to simply be a "should" statement of an underlying mistaken belief. The ones stemming from childhood experiences are the most stubbornly resistant to change.

In Kay's case, some of her FOOL Rules included, *I should:*

- *show off my money and the things it gets me.*
- *spend as much as possible now and ignore the future.*
- *worry and fret about money.*
- *give the man the financial power.*
- *put others' needs ahead of my own.*
- *live alone in order to prevent financial chaos.*
- *keep my money totally safe so that I don't have to worry.*

Kay remarked, "I **hate** worrying about money - **why** did I turn **that** into a rule for myself? I want to feel successful and harmonious about money, but it seems like no matter what I do, I torment myself with disturbing thoughts about it instead."

Kay remarked, "I *hate* worrying about money - why did I turn *that* into a rule for myself?"

Kay had become so accustomed to the tension about money in her years growing up, that without the familiarity of such tension she felt irresponsible and out of control. Fretting gave her back that "old familiar feeling" and a sense of control. Like the iceberg's mass of ice under the surface of the water, this had been invisible to Kay until she searched deep beneath the surface of her thoughts.

21

The Power in Your Money Personality

The rule inside Kay's rule seemed to be:

- *I should never ignore money or else it will all suddenly disappear.*

In exploring this further, Kay found that she had equated "harmony" about money with "ignoring" money. As extreme as this belief seemed at first, Kay realized it had been very real *to her*. She witnessed money suddenly disappearing over and over again in her childhood and concluded that the way to prevent that in her life was to actively monitor (and worry about) her money all the time. She had unconsciously rejected harmony because she believed it was dangerous. Kay feared she might wake up some morning and find her money had completely vanished.

Though Kay did want to feel more relaxed and harmonious about money, her fear of it vanishing had been greater than her desire to relax. She had unknowingly given the fear (of loss) greater power than the desire (for relaxation). Kay's habit of worrying about money followed her dominant emotion because she believed she couldn't be both relaxed (harmonious) and in control at the same time.

Kay began adjusting her habits

Kay redefined worry as a useless waste of imagination, and if it started, she labeled the worry and set it aside for her weekly planning meeting. She eliminated worry from her definition of responsible financial behavior.

Kay designated one evening a week as her planning meeting with herself. This is when she organized and paid her bills, reviewed her checking, savings, and investment accounts, and strategized to ease any worries that had come up. The rest of the week she "tabled" money thoughts.

Kay's list of "COOL Rules"

Kay also saw that some of her rules had cultural origins. The activity Kay did next was make a list of "societal shoulds" that came from her personal **Culture Of Origin Lessons (COOL Rules).** These are the messages Kay felt were sent directly and indirectly to her about money. Often these rules stem from perceptions of what behaviors are acceptable or desirable according to the group we are part of.

The slang expression, "Cool" in American society denotes pleasing or excellence. The problem is, if we rely exclusively on others' definition of whether we are cool or not, we can lose touch with our true selves. We become subject to similar misinterpretations as the FOOL and COOL rules combine and our behavior gets misdirected. You can see how Kay's COOL rules (below) had become the power in her money personality that steered her emotions and behavior in an unhelpful direction. They became like the tail that wagged the dog.

Some of Kay's personal COOL Rules had been, *I should:*

- *Spend all I make and charge the rest*
  (credit cards are cool)!

- *Borrow as much as the creditors allow me*
  (having it "all" now is cool).

- *Shop 'til I drop* (spending is cool).

- *Feel like a loser without the latest "toys"*
  (toys are cool).

- *[I must] Make more and more money to be successful*
  (a small income is uncool).

After becoming aware of her COOL/FOOL Rules, Kay began to see that money often mistakenly symbolized things external to her genuine value as a human being. This insight began with her examination of Flasher (the prestige spender) and the opposite personality, Stasher (the growth investor). Although one is the biggest saver (Stasher) and the other is the biggest spender (Flasher), money symbolizes **success** to both. The difference is how they *measure* success. Flasher measures it by the things money buys, while Stasher measures it by how impressively money grows.

The fiscal rascals also differ in the additional symbolic meanings they may give money. For example, Flasher may see money as a sign of power, esteem or love, whereas Stasher sees it as a sign of intelligence or excitement. There are a variety of things that money may symbolize for the other rascals as well, including greed, pleasure, conflict, importance, independence, freedom and security. Kay also visited Basher (the anti-materialism rascal) to gain ideas for being frugal and battling her urge to splurge.

Origin of COOL/FOOL Rules

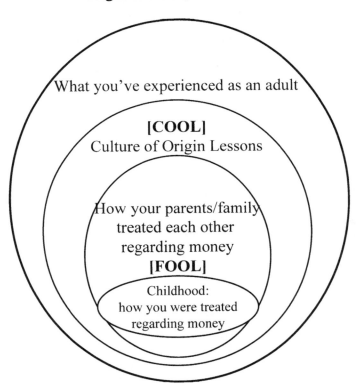

What you've experienced as an adult

[COOL]
Culture of Origin Lessons

How your parents/family
treated each other
regarding money
[FOOL]
Childhood:
how you were treated
regarding money

"Ghost busting" by talking back to the rascals

Another strategy Kay enjoyed was talking directly to her fiscal rascals when she felt one trying to pop up and sabotage her decisions. This light hearted "back-talk" renewed her confidence and control over her self-sabotaging urges. It externalized the forces that had misdirected some of her money behaviors in the past.

Kay could now visualize the character she was trying to tame. Without this external picture, it was like trying to tame a ghost. Not only was it impossible to see, the form and size it had was invisible. Now the habits she wanted to adjust had a defined form, with clear traits she could go to work on.

> ## Kay could now visualize the character she was trying to tame. Without this external picture, it was like trying to tame a ghost.

Some of Kay's comments to her Flasher rascal:

- *Oh, no you don't, Flasher. I know what you're up to and I won't let you steer me into overspending!*

- *Nice try, Flasher. But sorry, I don't need another new suit to feel successful at work.*

- *There you go tugging at me again, Flasher, but guess what? ? I'm going to let Stasher win this one. My bonus check is going to fund my IRA!*

Kay found this helped her reassert her new goals. Instead of feeling deprived or punished about the new choices she was making, she felt proud and rewarded. Kay had discovered there was something wonderful in each money rascal (refer to the Delightful/Frightful chart).

If any personality became overly dominant, however, it proved to be the underlying cause of financial stress and problems. By claiming and taming her fiscal rascals, Kay's urge to splurge kept in balance with her craving for saving. She began to make lasting changes in her financial habits. Kay experienced "money harmony" as her thoughts and actions came into alignment with her genuine goals.

Taming Your Fiscal Rascals

Aim to Tame, Not Maim!

Let's keep in mind the reason we have used the word "tame," is because we want to lessen the intensity of a fiscal rascal that has taken over one's money style and caused problems. We are **not** trying to completely extinguish or cripple (maim) any rascal.

Remember, there is something delightful in each one. If we try to completely disable the poor rascal, then we will lose. We will lose some of the delightful characteristics inherent in the rascal. And we may actually lose the battle by fanning the flame of the traits that we're trying to subdue.

The goal is to rebalance your mix of the eight types so that you can begin to solve the problems that an overly dominant one might have caused. Consider it a rascal re-allocation plan!

Claiming and Taming Your Bundle of Beliefs (BOB)

To begin taming any of the fiscal rascals, study the list of original beliefs for the specific rascal you want to tame. Remember, the original beliefs were likely formulated long ago, in a situation and at an age that no longer fits your current reality. And the old BOB is by definition, **invisible**. That is what makes taming such a challenging task.

Test each original belief of the rascal on yourself to determine if it fits for you. For example, the first one on the list for Flasher is "I am only as valuable as my possessions." It is possible that many of the original beliefs may at first strike you as not fitting, because your conscious philosophy is quite different. Your *intellectual* mind objects by saying, "Of course I don't believe that! Possessions are things - they aren't related to human value!"

But think more deeply and ponder emotions you have felt when observing "your stuff vs. their stuff" and you may discover beliefs that were present after all. Take a few moments to consider the multitude of societal and other messages that are fired at all of us every day. Advertising alone is enough to implant notions of personal failure for NOT acquiring certain products. The implications range from suggesting that "you are a rejected loser without this product," to "you cannot enjoy life to the fullest without it." Another message: You should feel deprived without it! These types of commercial messages can disturb your value systems and cause you to veer off track.

Be a PI of Your Beliefs' Presence Intensity (PI)

Be your own *private investigator* (PI) and give yourself a **"presence intensity" (PI) score of 1-10** for your beliefs. Ten means that relative to the statement, you think there is an extremely strong presence of the belief within you. Range your scoring down to one, for an extremely mild presence. If you are certain you never think this way, you may score it with a zero.

For example, to test the first item on Flasher's BOB (Bundle of Beliefs) list on yourself, ask the questions below.

_____ *Do I feel diminished in **any** way at the thought of doing without the things I want to buy?*

_____ *Do I compare my possessions or income to those of other people and use it as a gauge of my own success?*

_____ *Might I feel **inferior** to someone who DOES have the things that I do not have?*

_____ *How intense is that feeling? Subtle or significant? Does it result in a lowered sense of self worth?*

_____ *Do I feel better when I acquire these things and talk about or display them to others?*

_____ *How long does the better feeling last before it wears off and I need something new to refuel the good feeling? Hours? Days? Weeks?*

After you have gone through the original BOB list, add any other invisible beliefs that you have become aware of within yourself through these exercises. Score them on the 1-10 PI scale. For more information on how to discover your additional beliefs, go to the summary section, "Reviewing Fiscal Rascal Concepts."

Beware of "Sneakers"

The taming guide for each fiscal rascal is useful to review no matter what you claim as your dominant rascals. A stray belief from a rascal you haven't claimed may occasionally show up in another style. These stray beliefs have been nicknamed **sneakers**. They have a talent for sneaking into a place you don't expect them and orchestrating all kinds of mischief.

In some respects, "sneaker" is a good nickname for any belief that is nestled inside you, yet has cleverly managed to stay out of view. For that reason, it is helpful to inventory all of the listed beliefs from all rascals to catch any strays that may apply to you. As we have pointed out, the invisibility of any belief can steer you in a direction you may **not** want to go.

Without taking the first step of making an invisible belief *visible*, you may miss an important piece of your own unique BOB. By reviewing all of them, and adding any variety of your own, you will have a more complete picture of what you are tackling. That way you decrease the risk of a stray belief sneaking in from left field and sabotaging your entire effort.

Taming Thoughts: Old BOB vs New BOB

Study the list of the rascal's reconstructed beliefs. These are the corrected versions of the old mistaken beliefs. The problem with the old beliefs is that they are extreme, exaggerated, irrelevant, or just plain misfitting. Remember, the old beliefs originated from misinterpretations of earlier life events. They may contain "all or nothing" elements or "black and white" patterns.

Start with the items that had your highest PI (presence intensity) scores in the Old BOB section, rather than reading the new BOB list in order. Next, make any changes to the reconstructed beliefs to personalize it to you. Do this for all of the items scored above zero, starting with the highest and moving through to the lowest. Then write reconstructed beliefs for any other invisible beliefs that you have added to the list.

You have probably noticed that the reconstructed beliefs remove the extreme all-or-nothing component of the old BOB. They also separate the issue of human worth from financial score-keeping. Issues such as control, acceptance and love are separated from monetary factors. In essence, the new BOB is more positive and useful. By reconstructing the old damaging beliefs, you can begin to genuinely assess your deepest values and direct your life to be in harmony with them.

Once you have modified, added and studied the reconstructed beliefs of the rascal you want to tame, give yourself frequent exposure to them. Copy or rewrite them in several ways. Post these new and improved beliefs in areas you will see often.

Places to post the new beliefs:

Check register	desk
credit cards	dresser mirror
wallet	home's outside door
bathroom mirror	computer keyboard
under your pillow	underwear drawer
car dashboard	phone
refrigerator	calendar

The idea is to see the new beliefs frequently, repeat them out loud if you can and reaffirm your agreement with them. They are replacing old damaging beliefs that have been in place a long time and the old ones will fight to stay put. You need to be ready for that battle. The new reconstructed BOB is your combat gear and you will need it.

A powerful reinforcer of this is to share it with a trusted friend or advisor who can encourage you in times of doubt.

Take AIM (Act As If Modified)

One of the concepts for changing a problem behavior that will be listed for each rascal is the idea of acting as if you already **are** changed, or modified. That is what the AIM acronym "aims" at. The practice of engaging in modified behaviors that steer you toward the solution allows you to experience its beneficial aspects.

> **The practice of engaging in modified behaviors that steer you toward the solution allows you to *experience* its beneficial aspects.**

Remember there is something useful or delightful in each rascal. It's getting too much of a good thing that throws the rascal out of balance. That's when the **delightful** can turn into the **frightful**! You rebalance your style by practicing traits of other rascals that you lack.

Casher, the safe saver, for example, can actually benefit by "trying on" some of Rasher's tendencies "for size". The goal is to bring balance to the overall fiscal picture, not to switch one extreme behavior with another. We wouldn't want Casher to eliminate all caution and become a completely wild spender, totally impulsive and scattered with money. However, by setting aside a sliver of time and money to be impulsive and less controlled, Cashers can learn to enjoy spending a little more. This can help lift the veil of fear that "*everything* will fall apart" if they ever let go.

It's Time to Change *AIM*, Not to Find Blame

Another reason the AIM acronym is useful is that, as we pursue our personal growth and understanding, it gives us a crucial reminder about our beliefs. The objective is to uncover the mistaken interpretations and conclusions **we reached for ourselves** as a result of the experiences we had.

As we have seen, the underlying beliefs are one of the primary drivers of our actions, like a steering wheel that **aimed** us in a set direction. Studying our beliefs and how we came by them helps us understand and redirect our previously, sometimes faulty aim. We should **not** use these exercises to **blame** others for our beliefs or behaviors. The author of our beliefs is none other than ourselves.

Although some memories are difficult, unpleasant or painful, they do hold important information about our deeply held beliefs. You have the right to feel any of the emotions that may emerge when doing the work. But it will be counterproductive to your personal growth if you turn it into pursuit of blame, instead of pursuit of understanding your misdirected *aim*.

Please remember the arhymatherapy motto, *"It's time to change AIM, not to find blame!"*

Action Honoring Awareness (Aha!) Ideas

"Aha!" is an expression that exclaims an exciting insight. Uncovering invisible beliefs opens whole new worlds of awareness. The awareness that is gained can be exciting and insightful, as well as challenging. Unconscious thoughts look a little like the ostrich with its head in the sand - there's not much to see until it pops out and has a good look around. As much of our bundle of beliefs (BOB) had been unconscious, the tools needed to construct new mental and behavioral habits were missing.

Once you learn which invisible beliefs have been lurking in the murk, it becomes possible to tackle the misguided ones and try out adjustments to them. Reconstructing the misguided beliefs is the first action to take in order to honor the awareness gained.

Additional action ideas come from an examination of habits that have led to problematic outcomes. In each fiscal rascal section you will find ideas that are offered as **actions that honor the discoveries made** within the BOB.

That is the second meaning of Aha. Now that the beliefs can be seen, it's time to incorporate changes in actions so that your outcomes can improve. *That* aha looks more like the second ostrich in the review-chapter. It is important, also, to **visualize** the end goal and take each of the action steps to get there.

The Pain/Gain Ratio: Motivation to Change

One of the important factors in self change is related to what I call the **Pain/Gain ratio**. It is a way of factoring a person's perception of painful or difficult problems (pain) with the positive results (gain). Problems drain precious energy. It is up to each individual to determine if the pain and drain have become too great, thus motivating a change.

The theory, simply put, is that an individual is unlikely to make changes if the gain (perceived payoff) is greater than the pain (cost). Expressing this as a ratio with the costly pain factor on top and the gain at the bottom, can serve as a useful measure of a person's likelihood to initiate and maintain changes.

> **The theory, simply put, is that an individual is unlikely to make changes if the gain (perceived payoff) is greater than the pain (cost).**

Using a scale of 1-10 for each factor, let's look at how this would work:

The ratio is **pain over gain**, which we'll record as: **Pain/Gain.**

Mathematically, to change a ratio to a percentage or whole factor, you would divide the top number by the bottom number. For the purpose of this concept, call this resulting number the **pain factor (PF).**

Using this simple math as a guide, we can assess the degree of motivation to change. When someone identifies a behavior's resulting pain as *less than* (<) the gain (e.g., 4/8) for example, the numeric result is always less than 1. When the PF is less than 1, the likelihood of change is small. In effect, the individual perceives the price being paid (pain) is still "worth it" in order to get the result (gain).

What happens when the ratio is reversed? When the PF is *more than* 1 (>1 e.g., 8/4 = 2), the likelihood of change is greater. The greater the number exceeds 1, the more motivated the person is to change.

And what if the pain and gain ratings are equal? Using 4/4 as an example, four divided by 4 equals a PF of 1. When this happens and no "tie breaker" presents itself, the most likely result will be ambivalence and usually does not result in a change being made, at least not a significant or long lasting one.

That is because the sheer comfort of familiarity will be the unofficial tie breaker. Making a change carries with it a bundle of unknowns that may scare an ambivalent person off. Status quo, on the other hand, is a known entity and that creates a certain form of gain (familiarity), which keeps the person officially "stuck." They may *think* about changing, but they never actually do it.

> **An easy way to remember the meaning of the PF is that the bigger the number, the more likely one is to make a change.**

An easy way to remember the meaning of the PF is that the bigger the number, the more likely one is to make a change. It's a handy way to get a quick at-a-glance view of someone's motivation to change.

The Pain/Gain Pain Factor (PF) as a predictor of change:

> < 1 No change predicted (unmotivated)
> = 1 Change is unlikely (stuck/neutral)
> > 1 Likely to change (motivated)

About the Rascal Cases

Keep in mind that the cases represent examples of an extreme version of the rascal being described. Typically, however, there may be two or three rascals that combine to create any individual's unique and dominating money style.

The bundle of beliefs (BOB) listed in each case example present a range of possibilities exhibited by the rascal. There are many others that could be added. Feel free to modify the listed beliefs or add new ones to capture your own unique rascal style.

Notice the distortions of thought the beliefs contain:

- all-or-nothing thinking
- perfectionism
- fortune-telling
- catastrophizing
- exaggerations

All individual cases are unique and may have many additional invisible beliefs and sub-beliefs at work. Individuals should examine their own money history and modify the lists for maximum insight. Some rascals tend to routinely pair up with one another. Casher, the organized and controlled saver, commonly has a strong presence of Asher traits (the worrier). Therefore, when you review the rascals you have claimed as your own, look for their "companions" as well.

Now, let's get to know the individual fiscal rascals in detail!

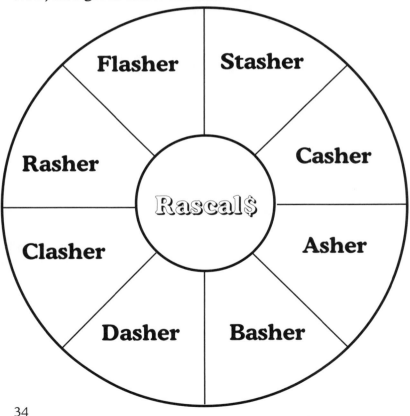

Rascal #1

Flasher

*Look here, I'm **Flasher** and I'm one cool cat.*
I am the one you should want to look at!
My toys are flashy, take lots of cashy--
Without them I'm afraid I might feel trashy!
When I show off I feel a little better,
Even if that makes me a major debtor!

Claiming Flasher

"Flashers" - urge to splurge on **flashy** purchases and depend on them to create a feeling and look of success. It has never occurred to them to resist their urge to splurge. Flashers represent the biggest image spenders of the group of rascals. To Flashers, splurge means lavish spending.

They enjoy the recognition, power, or attention they believe they are gaining. Flashers want to avoid humiliation or perceived social inferiority. They are the most opposite of Stasher. Both think big - but Flashers are the big-ticket *spenders* (vs. savers).

Flashers can be impulsive with a special fondness, for example, for impressive jewelry, Cadillacs and Beemers, the latest dual quad, positraction, dolby enhanced electronic equipment, elaborate lakeshore homes and all the latest gadgets for them, or Nino Cerruti suits and Laura Ashley gowns - whatever items Flashers believe create the appearance of social success or build their image.

The **look of success is the number one priority** for this rascal. Flashers may use money for power, and may feel inferior or unsuccessful without these external symbols of their worth. This personality is also very unlike Bashers, who seek to reject materialism and wealth for social image.

Flashers sometimes appear snobbish or competitive. They may show off or try to one-up the next guy, which may cause negative reactions with others. Often the worst problem overly dominant Flashers run into is the inability to *afford* the perpetual nature of their expensive splurging style.

Let's take a look at an extreme flasher.

Case History: Dee Luxe Flasher

Meet Dee Luxe Flasher. She knew what she wanted when it came to splurging. Dee wanted to earn more and more money so that she could supply her lifestyle with some *deluxe possessions*. Her habit was to buy as much as her available credit card limit would allow.

When Dee did save, it was only to build up a sum large enough to buy a more impressive home. Dee could hardly wait to move up from their original home, for it was far too modest for her taste. It didn't promote her successful image enough.

Dee felt deprived, restless and inferior living in such an ordinary place. Every time she was faced with a cost decision on her new home, she opted for the more lavish item. She was certain that when she moved into a larger home she would feel more contented.

Dee was a sales manager for a small manufacturing company. She enjoyed her leadership role, and she reasoned that because she was in such a visible role, her wardrobe had to be top notch and plentiful. This meant top department stores all the way. Dee saw every purchase as a necessity, even though some new suits hung in her closet with the tags still on them.

When she and her husband bought their new home, Dee was in her glory. It was brand new and hadn't been lived in before. She busied herself hiring a landscape artist to create the most beautiful yard. She was not satisfied with the quality of the toilets in the house, so within six weeks she had them torn out and replaced with the finest porcelain, technology and fixtures available.

Dee's eager friends gladly lined up to receive her cast offs. Often her "old" clothes were nicer than any of their new ones. But her generosity extended beyond giving away clothes - there were plenty of enthusiastic receivers of the "used" toilets that were replaced in her new home.

Her talent for finding the most upscale products was astonishing. No income came in unnoticed. She drove a luxury car, had plans for a boat and was booking a cruise when her boss entered her office on Tuesday and announced that the company had been sold and her position was eliminated.

Dee's last day of work would be today and she would receive no severance pay. Dee's husband had a good job, but her spending had elevated their lifestyle to a dependence on both incomes. The power in Dee's Flasher money personality had steered her into such out of control spending that this news was catastrophic.

The Dee Luxe Flasher profile

Let's first look at Flasher's profile, starting with her BOB. Remember, these are the bundle of beliefs she developed over her lifetime. Most of them have not been in her conscious awareness. They contain extremes and distortions of thought that have misguided her behavior. Notice the *italicized* words in the BOB lists. They represent rigid extremes or words that can have many different subjective interpretations. We'll look at the four types of money handling habits (PETS) typical of a flasher. Some sample COOL/FOOL rules that Dee established for herself due to her BOB will also be listed.

Flasher's Invisible and Distorted Bundle of Beliefs
(Original BOB in extreme)

1. I am *only* as valuable as my possessions.
2. I am a *failure* if I don't make a large income.
3. Others will think I'm successful only if I look *perfect*.
4. I am *superior* to others who have less money.
5. Buying the most expensive things makes me *worthwhile*.
6. Life is boring and meaningless without *lots* of luxuries.
7. If I *always* pick up the check, I am superior to my friends.
8. I have more *power* and get my way if I show off my money.

Flasher's *Physical* Habits of Handling Money

- Acquires and relies heavily on credit cards (if attainable).
- Spends any "extra" income quickly.
- Shops at prestigious stores.
- Eats at the finest restaurants.
- Carries a lot of cash if possible, especially big bills.
- Tends not to track expenses.
- Saves little or no money compared to spending.
- Has debt that may be growing faster than income.
- Purchase preferences tend to be prestigious cars, jewelry, high-tech equipment, clothes, homes, furnishings, vacations.
- Usually impulsively gives in to the urge to splurge.

Flasher's *Emotional* Habits With Money

When *spending,* Flasher temporarily FEELS:

Powerless (over urge to splurge)
Powerful (I can do this if I want to!)
Certain, urgent (I must get this)
Obsessed
Contented, gratified
Pleased, cheerful
Relieved from urge to splurge
Enthusiastic, purposeful
Important, successful
Elevated in self-esteem.
Competitive (Wait until they see this!)
Proud (of successful image)
Inspired (this is so cool!)

When *resisting spending,* Flasher FEELS:

Deprived	Defeated
Restless	Jealous (of others)
Bored	Lonely
Fidgety	Irritated
Frustrated	Discouraged
Depressed	Unsuccessful
Inferior	Bitter
Cheated	Empty
Disturbed	Angry

When *wrestling with debt* or other consequences, FEELS:

Overwhelmed	Exhausted
Confused	Inadequate, incompetent
Ashamed, guilty	Foolish
Tense, worried	Angry
Fearful, despairing	Blaming
Panicked	Victimized (it's not my fault)
Sad, low	Threatened, defensive
Isolated	Justified
Powerless (in ability to solve)	Humiliated (contradicts image)

Flasher's *Thought* Habits With Money

- Thinks about expensive things to buy next.
- Wants to look good, successful, powerful.
- Desires speed in buying decisions.
- Plans and visualizes where the purchases will be made.
- Rarely thinks about ability to afford the splurge.
- Thinks of immediate spending as the true purpose for money.
- Convinces self that savings can wait.
- Hates used items.

- Philosophies: You can't take it with you.
  I deserve this now.
  I'll worry about it later.
  Who cares?
  Everybody else does the same thing.
  I'll do better next month.
  Live for today.
  It's now or never!
  Go with your gut when it says, "Buy!"
  Spending is my reward for working.

Flasher's *Social* Habits With Money

- Seeks prestige, status, or image socially.
- Buys extravagant or unaffordable gifts for others.
- "Treats" others frequently (picks up the tab) when out socially.
- Attends social functions that may be unaffordable.
- Is vulnerable to peer pressure.
- Pays attention to what others have and do.
- Encourages others to participate in spending (let's go on a vacation together).
- Draws attention to purchases (show).
- Talks about purchases (tell).

COOL/FOOL Rules Flasher Mistakenly Created

- Continually add to your *deluxe* possessions (to prove personal value).
- Always wear the newest designer clothes (to prove *self-worth* to *everyone*).
- Pursue and achieve a *large income* (to feel successful).
- Use the same rigid *judgments* (to measure others' success).
- Feel like a *failure* if you don't achieve these things.

Taming Flasher

(Author's note: The taming strategies for all rascals have a number of things in common. Before proceeding, make sure you are familiar with the stragegies for change in the introduction - "Taming Your Fiscal Rascals.")

In the case of Dee Luxe Flasher, her immediate fiscal rascal challenge is taming her habit of big image spending. She not only has the task of paying for *past* expenditures, but needs to immediately curtail her *present* spending. The goal is to prevent future problems such as the one she is now faced with. Losing a job, like many high stress life events, can also serve as a positive catalyst for change.

Everyone faces multiple challenges when they lose their jobs as Dee has. A host of painful feelings such as failure, rejection, and victimization may emerge and there is much more to cope with than just the financial difficulties.

These other challenges would need to be identified and addressed, but are not within the scope of the Fiscal Rascals taming guide being presented in this work. The assumption is that these additional needs would be integrated with the fiscal rascal taming strategies to effect a holistic solution.

Reconstructing Flasher's Bundle of Beliefs

In order to put her life back in order after losing her job, Dee needs to accept the fact that her dominant fiscal rascal has been Flasher. She needs to do something to tame that rascal. She starts by reconstructing her BOB to look more like this:

Flasher's Bundle of Beliefs (Original BOB in extreme)	Flasher's Reconstructed Beliefs (New Goals)
1. I am only as valuable as my possessions.	1. I am valuable separate from and regardless of my possessions.
2. I am a failure if I don't make a large income.	2. I am a success no matter what the size of my income is.
3. Others will think I'm successful only if I look perfect.	3. I am successful even when I look imperfect.
4. I am superior to others who have less money.	4. Money is not a measure of human inferiority or superiority.
5. Buying the most expensive things makes me worthwhile.	5. I am worthwhile regardless of how expensive my things are.
6. Life is boring and meaningless without lots of luxuries.	6. Life is as exciting and meaningful as I want, with or without lots of luxuries (or money).
7. If I always pick up the check, I am superior to my friends.	7. True friends are equals, neither superior nor inferior.
8. I have more power and get my way if I show off my money.	8. Using money to get my way deprives me of more meaningful relationships.

In privately investigating the invisible and reconstructed beliefs, Dee can test them out for their PI (presence intensity). In Dee's case, she claimed that all eight beliefs listed were present in her to some degree. She gave each one a 1-10 PI rating and found that her most prevalent beliefs were, "I am only as valuable as my possessions" and "I am a failure if I don't make a large income."

Dee found great relief in reviewing the reconstructed beliefs, especially "I am valuable separate from and regardless of my possessions." Dee studied the BOB lists and modified them to fit some of her unique twists on the themes, and kept copies in several places.

Can Dee Luxe Flasher change?

Let's begin to address the question, "Can Dee Luxe Flasher change?" To a non-spending personality type, Dee's adjustment would appear to be a breeze. But to Dee, it is her **perception of success** that has been threatened by her loss of job and income. Her definition of success has been coming from her external display of material things. The more she acquired, the more she needed to acquire in order to fill the emotional void. Much like other addictions, the spending that once satisfied Dee, no longer did. It took more and more material goods to help Dee feel relief from her urge to splurge. This phenomenon happened gradually enough that Dee was not aware it was occurring.

One of Dee Flasher's first reactions to losing her job would most likely be, "I have to hurry up and get a new job!" The problem, as she would perceive it initially, is about *income*, not *outflow*. Put another way, Dee would not immediately see her spending as part of the problem. As far as she's concerned, *deluxe* spending is the reason you have a job. And you need a good one in order to have *deluxe* purchasing power. "Isn't that what everybody's after?" she wondered.

Dee has mistaken purchasing power for personal power. Despite how obvious this would be to controlled spenders, the idea of changing her spending habits would not occur to Dee in the immediate crisis.

But there are other forces at work that won't let Dee ignore the spending problem for long.

The three major reality forces in Dee 's case are:

1. *Dee's marriage is at risk due to her spending.*
2. *Dee cannot get a new job fast enough to cover her bills.*
3. *The creditors want to be paid on time.*

These forces will modify Dee's field of vision and force her to look at her spending habits. In this instance, the needed change is identified as, "Reducing Dee's spending." What will Dee Flasher need in order to make a change that she can maintain?

The Pain/Gain Ratio for Dee Luxe Flasher

1. Dee's marriage is at risk due to her spending.

In Dee's case, she does care about her relationship with her husband, Lee. The fact that he is extremely upset is painful to her. In fact it is now a major drain because she's never seen him this bothered. Although her job loss is not the first time Lee has questioned or complained about her spending, it does seem to be the first time Dee has *heard* his complaints.

Although she has always been aware of what she thinks she gained from her spending (fine quality material goods, excitement, prestige, etc.), she's been unaware of the pain. Of course, there are many problems that create emotional pain when overspending is extensive and chronic. But the only one that is catching Dee's attention so far is the relationship problem. It has upset her Pain/Gain ratio.

Before Dee lost her job, she felt differently about Lee's complaints. The gain still outweighed the pain. She wasn't happy about Lee's complaints, but it was a price she was willing to pay in order to have her way with spending. The ratio when still employed was $4/10 = .4$ pain factor (PF). With a ratio of less than 1, the likelihood of a change in Dee's flashy and lavish spending patterns was low.

Now, however, Lee is threatening divorce. He wants a plan that permanently solves this financial problem. Lee has wanted a plan for a long time, but until now he tolerated Dee's excuses and procrastination. With the mounting debt and only one income (his), he will no longer take the back seat to their financial decisions. Lee has drawn the line: either they go to a counselor, or he leaves the marriage.

What is Dee's Pain/Gain ratio now? Her pain rating just shot up to a 10. When faced with losing Lee, the gain she thought she was getting from all her spending paled by comparison. She didn't realize her spending had been so stressful to him. Her marriage was more important than her "deluxe stuff." Her new ratio was 10/8 = 1.25 PF. Although this was not a strong motivation to change, at least she had moved out of the unmotivated range. But there are two more forces about to come into play.

2. Dee cannot get a new job fast enough to cover her bills.

What *would* be fast enough for Dee? Right now! Today! In her situation, Dee can't afford to lose a single day's pay (in fact, she could use a second job). Unfortunately, her urgent need does not match up with reality. Dee doesn't even have a resume and it's been years since she has been job hunting. She's not sure what her marketable skills are - after all, her company let her go.

If she had been a more valuable employee, she wonders, would she still have a job? Dee's not sure anymore. She will have to get going on her resume, but what else? No matter what Dee thinks to add to her new crisis-driven "to-do" list, the timetable for landing a new job is **not** going to meet her immediate financial needs. Her Pain/Gain ratio about spending is now changing again.

Part of Dee's BOB is that she must earn a large income in order to be worthwhile. With her income at exactly zero, and no job prospects on the immediate horizon, she feels like a total failure. Dee now rates her emotional upheaval from splurging as high (pain), while her perceived benefit (gain) from all her expenditures is shrinking. Her new ratio is 8/4, for an elevated PF of 2.

3. The creditors want to get paid on time.

Dee had been so good at deluxe spending that she completely neglected saving. This leaves her with the double-whammy of having no emergency money on reserve to cushion the blow of being without an income. The thought of not being able to pay the household bills is in conflict with Dee's successful image. With two incomes, she could usually pay all their fixed living expenses and make at least the minimum payments due on their credit cards. But now her household's total monthly outflow exceeds the inflow. She doesn't know what happens when you can't make the required payments.

Dee's fear of the unknown escalates rapidly and she starts to visualize profound humiliation over her inability to pay the bills. Will the creditors call her former company looking for her? She worries they will tell her former coworkers that she is in debt. She wonders if there really are debtors prisons out there. Now her PF has exceeded the previous two calculations. The pain of such humiliation has risen to a 10, while her gain drops to a 2. Dee has broken her own record for a pain factor - she is now all the way up to a PF of 5.

Dee Flasher is now motivated to change, as seen by her average PF score which is greater than 1, but it took a crisis (job loss) to cause the movement. The long term challenge will be for Dee to retain some of the new behaviors even after she finds a job again. A danger Flashers have is that once the crisis fades away, so does the motivation to reform. For this reason, Dee needs to review the taming strategies in the introductory chapter, and do the exercises using the BOB list of beliefs, both invisible and reconstructed.

Flasher's AIM: Changing and Balancing Habits

Dee needs to practice doing different behaviors, by acting **As If Modified** already. The fact that she is experiencing severe problems indicates that many of the habits listed for Flasher have proven to be a disservice to her.

First, she needs to go through the list and check off the items that do apply to her. The best way to make use of the list, is for Dee to think of an alternative that seems to state the opposite of what her tendencies have been, and practice doing them.

For example, one item on the list of *Flasher's Physical Habits of Handling Money* is, "Acquires and relies heavily on credit cards." Dee has checked that item as applying to her, and she rewrites the habit that she needs to acquire as, "Uses cash only for purchases." This emphasizes a rejection of the use of credit and Flashers need to act as if they have already modified their habit, by engaging in new and more useful ones. Another example of taking a new AIM for Dee is that instead of spending income *quickly,* she will work on establishing the opposite habit of spending it *slowly.*

Dee will use the list of emotional habits for Flasher to reframe how she feels. Instead of feeling pleased and important when spending, for example, she will congratulate herself and strive to feel pleased and important for *resisting* spending.

> **Dee will use the list of emotional habits for Flasher to reframe how she feels.**

Flasher Visiting Other Rascals

Another strategy that Dee may find useful in helping her achieve balance, is to review the lists of habits for rascals that seem to be the opposite of the one causing her problems. Since Flasher is at the far end of spending, for example, Dee should review the habits of savers to look for new behaviors to act on.

Action Honoring Awareness (Aha!) Ideas

Cancel and return: Dee will need to cancel any major expenditures she had been planning on (cruise, buying a boat, if the deluxe toilets aren't yet installed, return them, and return any other non-essential items that can be. The clothing in the closet with tags still attached is an example of this).

It is helpful if the couple can work together on a problem by "tackling" it with mutual energy, rather than blaming one or the other. Dee and Lee can work together to comprise a list of monthly fixed and variable expenses, so that they know the required outflow that they are dealing with. They can use the "Monthly Bills Ledger," (see Appendix) to list what they owe each month, and record the amounts due and payments as they're made.

Make lists: Staying away from shopping centers and other areas that trigger her urge to splurge, is one practice Dee will need to exercise. And when she does go, Dee should shop with a list of necessary items that is prepared ahead of time. She and Lee still need to eat and sticking to a list of planned items at the grocery store will help them lower their food bill. Shopping for food is not the primary problem behind a Flasher's typical debt, but the grocery store *is* a good place to practice resisting impulse buys. It is also a great place to practice comparison shopping. These are critical new habits for Flashers to acquire.

Walletless shopping: If Dee does have to go into a shopping center for a needed item, she would be best served if she went without her wallet. She needs to remove all possibility of making an unplanned purchase by being "empty handed" when a desirable item or the urge to splurge appears. No cash, credit cards or checkbook is allowed in the store. This helps her resist the temptation to buy so that she can "escape" the mall splurge-free.

If the item Dee has found is on her list, she can note the price next to the item. She needs to go home before making a spending decision so that she has a cooling off period to remind her of her higher priority goals. She can then double check her inventory to determine how genuine the need is for her listed item.

Written plan and savings: When the immediate crisis of unemployment is solved, Dee should keep a written spending plan to help her stay within her means. Part of the spending plan should include her emergency fund and her "Future Successful Self." This latter category in an ordinary budget might be called "retirement" but to Dee that may seem too intangible and far off.

This also recognizes that Dee's desire to look and feel successful is not likely to swing all the way to wanting to look noble and poor. One of the most important reasons Dee has for beginning to save for the future is to maintain her financial dignity. If she continues to overspend her income during her working years, she will suffer considerably later on.

Budgeting indulgences: Another way for Dee to contain her spending in the future without feeling totally deprived, is to set aside a portion of each check for prestige items. This way she can still see that she can include some of this in her plan, rather than having to eliminate it all together. The difference between this and her former habit is in the planning and frequency of the splurge.

Dee will not be able to continue with constant home upgrading, but she can still accumulate portions of money over time to purchase an item just for the "niceness" of it.

Without acknowledging some of this need, the spending plan might begin to feel like too strict a diet. Having to give up ice cream for ever and ever, for example, may trigger an *eating* binge. A spending plan that's too strict for a recovering Flasher could trigger a "shop-til-you-drop" *spending* binge. This would obviously cause further unwanted financial damage.

Journal it: To help increase Dee's retention of contained spending habits, she should also keep a journal of items she has had thoughts of buying. This can be done on a yellow pad, spiral notebook, or a journal. I recommend using the cheapest method possible as a first step for Flashers to experience the reality of how effective a simple, low cost method can be. Otherwise, Dee's first reaction to keeping a journal might be to choose something that's leather-bound, gold-plated and engraved! Instead, she should keep it very simple: write the date at the top left of the page, and then list each thing she thinks of buying for a period of at least one week. Put the price range of the item next to it.

Dee should then note any particular emotion felt at the thought of having the item. Put an **"I"** (for image) next to the item if part of the appeal is image, or one of feeling good in some way because of how others may regard her for having it. The "I's" represent the presence of Flasher beliefs that could sabotage her efforts to contain her old spending habits. They also serve as an indicator of how alert and on guard she needs to be relative to her old tendencies taking over her decision making.

She will write the symbol **"$"** next to the item if she has to use credit cards or loans of some kind to acquire it. This will be especially important to Dee while she is unemployed, because just about anything she might think of buying will require credit. The dollar sign serves as a reminder of her true inability to afford the item.

Next, Dee will note any emotional reaction she has when she thinks of depriving herself of the item. She will check to see if it matches others on the Flasher list of emotional habits with money. This is another way of measuring the existence of Flasher's tendencies, so that her need to stay on guard will remain in her thoughts. Considering Dee's past history, she will need to be on guard for quite some time.

Flasher Celebrates AIM and Aha Successes

One of the most important components of retaining new and improved habits is remembering to notice and celebrate even the smallest changes. Flasher, like all of the Fiscal Rascals, should keep a separate daily **P**ositive **A**ccomplishment **T**hankful (PAT) journal. This is one way that Dee Flasher has of remembering to give herself a PAT on the back for sticking with desirable changes. This can be recorded on a small calendar or tablet to capture the positive successes she is experiencing in her new behaviors.

Reinforcing and paying attention to the benefits derived from the new behaviors is critical to combating old habits that may be trying to fight their way back into her financial personality. Dee, for example, might feel deprived if it weren't for her PAT journal listing her successes at resisting spending.

Summary of Taming Strategies for Flasher

♦ Claim the old beliefs that have misguided you.
♦ Reconstruct them to create new, useful beliefs.
♦ Claim and tame any sneakers that have strayed into your BOB.
♦ Set aside time to organize your financial responsibilities.
♦ Assess the Pain/Gain ratios.
♦ Visit the other rascals for tips and incorporate new behaviors from them for a greater balance of habits.
♦ Make note of all progress and celebrate it as you go.
♦ Establish a financial plan that helps define healthy financial boundaries for your short term and long term goals.

Rasher

*Say hi to **Rasher**, I love impulse buys,*
Right through my fingers money usually flies!
I think a budget is a mighty pest,
It takes away my fun and spending quest!
I care the most about my here and now,
Plan for the future? I would not know how!

Claiming Rasher

"Rashers" urge to splurge *frequently*, though not on such lavish items as Flashers. They are almost the opposite of Cashers, because the *last* thing they want to do is "squirrel away" money. Known for making **rash** and impulsive decisions with money, Rashers' spending is like the mechanical bunny - it keeps going and going and going. . . Rashers love the experience of shopping - the stimulation of looking, choosing, buying and possessing new items. To Rashers, "splurge" means *frequent* indulgence of their shopping desires.

Rashers often spend money on themselves and/or others whether they can afford it or not and may be in debt as a result. Rashers dislike saving, budgeting, planning and tracking expenses. If Rashers *do* save any money, it's usually kept liquid so that it can be retrieved for spending desires that may arise. Goal setting and interest in the future is a low priority to Rashers.

Case History: Max Rasher

Meet Max Rasher. Of all the hobbies, recreation, and relaxation activities out there, Max found shopping suited his urge to the *max.* He worked for a small company as a project coordinator. It was a good job that gave him adequate income for basic needs and then some. Max said he didn't need titles and prestige. What he liked was the variety of tasks he had at work. He felt it would be boring otherwise. He didn't have to put in heroic hours for job security, and his free time was something he valued.

Though he valued his free time, Max usually didn't make plans. If he was invited somewhere, he would usually go and have a good time. He spent freely on whatever seemed to fit the mood at the time. Max also liked camping and fishing, but he found it difficult to actually get plans made for excursions to area lakes.

The easiest excursion he found to occupy himself in his free time was to the local shopping malls. His favorite items to shop for were related to fishing and camping. This included everything from inexpensive novelty T-shirts to fishing and camping equipment and gadgets. Max found himself wandering through sporting goods and related departments of stores and malls every weekend and many evenings when he got bored with TV at home. The more he wandered, the more things he found.

Most of the equipment was stored in his shed. He liked his "stuff." It didn't matter that he couldn't possibly use it all. Looking at all of the latest equipment gave him a thrill unmatched by even the most exciting episode of his favorite television show. The search was entertaining and the "click" he felt inside when he found something he admired made his urge to splurge seem irresistable.

During his shopping excursions, Max developed a fondness for wildlife art. At first his collection was limited to fishing scenes. But it soon moved to black bears, then on to wolves. He couldn't resist adding to his collections. Before long, his fascination was non-discriminating. Loons, raccoons, ducks, deer, rabbits, cougars and wolves all became "fair game" for his splurging habit.

When he ran out of wall space for his paintings and prints, he began collecting pottery figurines. When he ran out of shelving for his figurines, he shopped for more shelves. That gave him a purpose for shopping. He sometimes wondered about moving into a larger place, but that took a lot of planning, which was quite unappealing to Max.

No single item in his collection would have been considered a major purchase. But the sheer *quantity* of items Max was buying began to take a significant financial toll. His income couldn't keep up with his shopping. When the checking account emptied, there were always credit cards to fill the gap. At first it was simple for Max to pay more than the minimum due on his credit cards, but as the balances grew, so did the minimum payments.

Before he knew it, Max could no longer keep up with the minimum amounts due. He began skipping payments, but the bills kept coming. Then the collection phone calls started. The more stressed Max felt about this problem, the more he felt like shopping. He would resist one weekend, then "*max* out" by the next one. He still got the thrill from searching for, finding and buying things, but it was short lived. The thrill was quickly substituted with fear and shame as his inability to keep up with his expenses worsened. Max felt cheated, persecuted and incapable of solving the problem.

Max was in **max**imum debt. The power in his Rasher money personality had misdirected him into indiscriminate, frequent spending that had become destructive. The pain had become greater than the gain. Now what?

The Max Rasher profile

Once again we'll look at Rasher's profile, starting with his BOB. Remember, these are the bundle of beliefs he developed over his lifetime, and he is unaware of most of them. *Italicized* words point out the distorted or subjective aspect of the mistaken belief. Then we'll look at the four typical money handling habits (PETS) of a rasher. Next, some of Rasher's COOL/FOOL Rule creations will be listed.

Rasher's Invisible and Distorted Bundle of Beliefs
(Original BOB in extreme)

1. Life is fun *only* if I'm spending *all* my money.
2. Saving money is *boring* and *impossible*.
3. I'm a *failure* if I can't spend my money on *all* things I want.
4. Debt is *always* the American way!
6. I deserve to be impulsive with *all* my money.
7. I don't care about the *future*.
8. People *love* me more when I give them gifts.

Rasher's *Physical* Habits of Handling Money

- Is impulsive about buying decisions.
- Frequents shopping malls and large multi-purpose stores such as Target or Walmart.
- Spends considerable free time shopping, looking, and buying.
- May use shopping catalogs and TV shopping channels.
- Purchases may not be expensive, but are high in *frequency*.
- May look for special sales and discounts as incentive to buy more.
- Stocks up when excited, regardless of need or affordability.

- Has no budget.
- Keeps minimal or no record keeping of expenditures.
- Irregularly pays bills, is nonsystematic, may be chaotic.
- Uses credit cards and is likely to be in debt.
- May go shopping to buy one item, but also purchases several unrelated, unneeded and unplanned items.

Rasher's *Emotional* Habits With Money

When *spending,* Rasher temporarily FEELS:

Stimulated, high	Carefree
Excited, elated	Busy, entertained
Satisfied	Purposeful
Happy	Out of control (over urges)
Urgent	Vulnerable
Relieved (from boredom)	Sneaky, naughty

When *resisting spending,* Rasher FEELS:

Low	Dissatisfied	Confused
Uneasy	Irritable	Conflicted
Cheated	Disconnected	Pressured
Bored	Sad	Trapped

When *wrestling with debt* or other consequences, FEELS:

Cheated	Embarrassed
Defensive	Foolish
Isolated, lonely	Upset, distraught
Childish	Distracted
Incapable	Persecuted
Helpless	Rejected
Abandoned	Vulnerable

Rasher's *Thought* Habits With Money

- Thinks about shopping in general.
- Believes life is dull unless spending or planning to spend.
- Doesn't think about savings or the future.
- Thinks something is wrong if the money isn't all spent.
- Has the belief that debt is normal.
- Hates thinking about getting organized or having constraints on spending.
- Thinks the purpose of work is for splurging.
- Philosophies: See Flasher.

Rasher's *Social* Habits With Money

- Seeks fun and excitement with money.
- Is usually very active, on the go, likes "going out" with friends.
- Gets quickly bored when items aren't new, especially in group activities.
- Wants to be included in action regardless of cost.
- May be attracted to and engage in gambling.
- Enjoys giving gifts as another reason to shop.
- "Treats" others to please or gain affection.

COOL/FOOL Rules Rasher Mistakenly Created

- I need to spend *all* of my money in order to believe life is *fun*.
- *Never* save any money.
- *Always* be impulsive with money to feel happy.
- *Never* do *any* future financial planning.
- Use money for gifts in return for *love*.

Taming Rasher

(Author's note: The taming strategies for all rascals have a number of things in common. Make sure you are familiar with the strategies for change in the introduction - "Taming Your Fiscal Rascals.")

Rasher's runaway splurging has created a monster in his life. His only recourse is to accept his rascal and begin to find balance. He starts by reconstructing his BOB.

Reconstructing Rasher's Bundle of Beliefs

Max reviewed the list of Rasher's original and reconstructed BOB and found some degree of truth in all of them.

Rasher's Bundle of Beliefs (Original BOB in extreme)	Rasher's Reconstructed Beliefs (New Goals)
1. Life is fun only if I'm spending *all* my money.	1. Life is more fun when some of my activities do not involve spending.
2. Saving money is boring and impossible.	2. Saving money is smart, energizing and possible!
3. I'm a failure if I can't spend my money on things I want.	3. I am successful when I make wise spending decisions.
4. Debt is the American way!	4. Debt is the troublesome way!
5. Shopping is always the best way to reward myself.	5. Shopping is seldom the best way to reward myself.
6. I deserve to be impulsive with *all* my money.	6. I deserve to be in balance with my money.
7. I don't care about the future.	7. I care about the older person I will someday be.
8. People *love* me more when I give them gifts.	8. People love me for who I am, not for what I give them.

At first Max didn't like admitting the existence of beliefs such as, "I deserve to be impulsive with all my money" (#6 on the BOB list). But when he used the 1-10 PI scale (presence intensity), he thought about the almost ritualistic stages his shopping trips would go through, starting with an "urge to splurge."

Right at the point of purchase he realized he had defined the item as something he deserved if he felt excited about it. The thought of affordability ceased to be a factor and out came the credit card. Belief #6 was true for Max, after all. He went from reacting initially with a PI of zero to the maximum rating of ten.

This issue of *deserving-ness* was especially true for Max because he found that there were predictable events that triggered his urge to splurge. Stress was one of the feelings that pulled that trigger for Max. Shopping had a calming effect on him and in his stressed feeling, he felt he needed an external scratch to ease the internal, emotional itch. Buying something for himself had turned into that "scratch." And once he gave in to the shopping urge, the search was guaranteed to result in a purchase.

For Max, it was as though shopping were a single motion that had to end in a purchase. This result occurred in spite of the fact that most of the calming effect actually took place in the browsing stage.

Although Max hadn't thought of his collecting as impulsive before, he could now see the impulsive element of it. He had mistakenly identified his collection (wildlife items) as a planned expense.

The ex-wife specter

After all, Max rationalized, he wasn't out grabbing new clothes and ten dozen pairs of shoes like his ex-wife used to do. He had unconsciously written himself a permission slip to collect all of the wildlife items he wanted regardless of the cost. To his dismay, it began to look more similar to the behaviors of his ex-wife than he originally thought. Both had created debt by purchasing items they did not genuinely need and could not use.

Max also noticed that the debt he had accumulated seemed separate and unattached to the items he had purchased to create it. His enjoyment of the purchases had ended long before the bill even showed up. Now he was faced with this enormous amount of money owed, but couldn't put his finger on any benefit it was currently bringing him. The debt felt like an unfair burden because he wasn't receiving any real enjoyment from the items that created it in the first place.

Fun doesn't have to require spending

Max realized that he had also had a high PI score for belief #1, "Life is fun only if I'm spending *all* my money." Max found that boredom had been one of the triggering feelings that sent him shopping. He had also equated success with spending impulsively, which misled him to buying things frequently in order to feel successful. Max felt relieved at the reconstructed belief, "Life is more fun when some of my activities *don't* involve spending."

> **He had also equated success with spending impulsively, which misled him to buying things frequently in order to feel successful.**

It was as though this hadn't occurred to Max before. He began making a list of activities he could do that would *not* have an expense. He thought of things he did for fun as a kid and built from that. One of his favorite outings as a child, for example, had been going to the big park in town and having family picnics. He had wonderful memories of playing Frisbee with his cousins.

Thinking about how much he had enjoyed it reminded him of something else: *you need a buddy to play Frisbee.* Max was suddenly aware of how isolated and alone he had become as a frequent shopper. For Max, this explained some of the empty feelings he had begun to experience more and more frequently. He had stopped socializing due to his overuse of shopping as a free time activity.

He decided to get more involved in community recreation and other activities that cost little or nothing, yet would bring socialization back into his life. Instead of rewarding himself with shopping, he was going to reward himself with activities that had the added benefit of meeting new people.

The problem with Max Rasher is that his habit of frequent shopping splurges has *maxed* out credit cards, his checking account credit and his overall capacity to pay for the items. The financial problems faced by Max look similar to Dee Flasher's debt, but the spending habits that got him there were not the same.

Max bought multiples of certain material goods because of the pleasure the whole experience created for him, whereas Dee was seeking prestige and image. Max's shopping turned into a problem because of the sheer *frequency* of his purchases, whereas Dee got into trouble because of the *size* of her purchases.

Max is quite impulsive about his spending and he is caught in a cycle of "going with" his sensations and urges as he shops, rather than thinking through any practicality or affordability about the material goods that grab his attention. In the case of both Max Rasher and Dee Flasher, material goods have caused such a financial problem that they should be renamed, "material bads."

> **In the case of both Max Rasher and Dee Flasher, material goods have caused such a financial problem that they should be renamed, "material bads."**

Now faced with debts that he was unable to keep up with, and still saddled with the habit of shopping that created the situation in the first place, Max felt childish and incapable of solving his problem. Like other Rashers, Max had done the spending so unconsciously, that the enormity of the problem actually came as a surprise to him.

His financial organization was void of any comprehensive view of the big picture, so Max had been able to mount debt without ever being aware of its size. Max not only needed help getting organized, but also with combating his urge to splurge, especially when under stress.

It has been said that people are like tea bags - when put in hot water, that's when you find out what's inside. This is certainly true of the money rascals. They are most likely to display their frightful traits in times of stress. But by taming them and creating more balance of the mix, better reactions to stressful periods can protect finacial security.

The Pain/Gain Ratio for Max Rasher

The very surprise that Max experienced at his inability to keep up with his spending was an indication of how he was able to create the problem to start with. By only looking at a tiny sliver of his financial picture at a time, Max was able to fool himself into believing that each purchase resulted in gain with no pain.

If he bought a wildlife painting for $200, for example, he would think of it in an isolated way, as if $200 was the only money he had spent, or ever would spend. Each purchase "felt" affordable then, because he didn't add it to all the other items he had added to his collection in the last two weeks. In truth, the $200 was only one tenth of the purchases he had made since his last paycheck. The nine other items were sitting on a credit card with a new purchase balance of $2000, and a growing balance of $9800 plus interest from previous months.

By splurging in ignorant bliss, Max reported a Pain/Gain ratio of 4/10. With a PF of less than 1 (4 divided by 10), Max fell into the "no motivation to change" category. However, the ratio began to change when the credit card companies that had been receiving erratic payments turned his accounts over to their collection department. The collection callers recited over and over again what the balances had grown to. These large sums seemed like shocking amounts to Max and for the first time he could see that he could no longer afford all the spending he had been doing.

Now the pain (and drain) of the debt exceeded the joy (gain) of the "material bads" he had so excitedly collected. The changed ratio was now 10/2, for a PF of 5. His motivation to change had just increased nearly six-fold. Max wanted to know what to do next.

Rasher's AIM: Changing and Balancing Habits

Max Rasher needs to practice several new behaviors, including shopping that does not end in making a purchase. In studying the BOB, Max became aware of his problematic definition of shopping, as shopping = buying. Max wanted to be able to shop occasionally without having it turn into additional debt. Like Dee, he would limit his shopping trips and leave his wallet, credit cards and checkbook at home.

As a way of helping Max, we nicknamed shopping centers "Money Museums." This way, he could go to look at the "interesting displays" and get enjoyment from just viewing them. Max changed his focus of shopping *from* "looking to own" *to* "looking to look." To a non-spender type, this may sound like an obvious action, but to Max it was a new idea.

Max reviewed the lists of typical habits of Rasher and focused especially on the *Physical Habits of Handling Money* to identify behaviors to change. Using the AIM strategy of Acting **As If M**odified, Max decided to try out the opposite of being impulsive about buying decisions. He would practice this by identifying something the Rasher rascal would have wanted to buy and then reflect on it instead of acting on his urge to splurge. Max decided to give his new goals more power than his old urge to splurge.

One way Max did this was by listing questions he could ask himself about the true value and usefulness of the item. For the first time ever, **Max began to ask questions such as:**

- *Where will I put this item?*
- *Will I be able to use it enough?*
- *Is there some lower cost or no cost way to have it?*
- *In what way will I use it?*
- *How often will I use it?*
- *How much will I truly enjoy it?*
- *Will the cost take away from my other goals?*
- *How many hours do I have to work to pay for it?*
- *If I don't get this, will I forget about it a week from now?*
- *How much is this money worth if I saved it or applied it to debt instead of spending it?*

Much like the other spender, Flasher, Max also used the list of emotional habits to identify new feelings to strive for to pair with new beliefs. Now, instead of feeling excited when spending, he felt excited when choosing an alternative behavior from his list. One of his new goals was to participate in community activities. Instead of feeling *out* of control, he felt *in* control.

Rasher Visiting Other Rascals

Max visited Casher and Stasher to "shop" for additional goals of new behavior about money. The physical habits were the ones he chose to focus on from Casher, striving to become debt free, organized and on time with bills, having savings, and knowing the big picture.

Max also wanted to elevate the importance of savings. The visit to Casher and Stasher gave Max much to work on. The most urgent task was to get organized with his financial affairs. Understanding the beliefs behind his problematic behaviors would help Max have greater emotional control over his spending. Having a clear view of the big picture of his financial world would help Max put his spending in perspective so that he couldn't fool himself like he used to.

Action Honoring Awareness (Aha!) Ideas

As we have seen, there is some similarity between the problems of Max Rasher and Dee Flasher. In some ways however, Max has it easier, because his fixed expenses are not as enormous as Flasher's are. Dee Flasher has a large, expensive home accompanied by an equally large, expensive mortgage payment. Max, on the other hand, never got out of control with his basic lifestyle habits. He simply bought other "stuff" too often, acquiring many non-essential smaller ticket items.

Tame frequent spending: Unlike Flasher, Max doesn't have any large items he can return or cancel and he does still have an income generating job. The primary habit Max will tame is the frequency of his spending trips. Max will start making lists of items he needs (or wants) and reflect on them before making any decisions.

Debt repayment: Max will establish a spending plan for repayment of debt and his fixed expenses. Max will apply for a home equity loan to consolidate his debts on a tax-preferred basis. If he can't do that, he will look for lower interest credit cards, starting with the ones on which he currently has a balance and will consolidate as much of the total debt as possible to a lower interest rate card(s).

63

Max will pay as much as he can on the highest interest rate debt first and will work his way down to the lowest interest rate debt until he is debt free. New purchases will be made with budgeted cash only, not credit cards.

Schedule organizing time: Max will schedule his financial organizing time, so that it becomes a habit. Max will record his bills on the "Monthly Bills Ledger," (see Appendix), so that he has a reference for when things are due, as well as a gauge of the progress he is making as he goes along. Just as Flasher allowed herself a prestige purchase in the spending plan, Max will have a category for "impulse buys."

Again, without letting some part of the Rasher style live on, Max could end up feeling too restricted and go on a binge shopping excursion. The key factor, however, is that the dollar amount available for impulse buys is quite modest, especially while Max is paying off the previously accumulated debt.

Journal it: Max should keep a journal like the one described for Flasher. That way, when an urge to splurge hits, instead of acting on it, Max can add it to the list and note significant information about it. Like Flasher, Max will need to see the **"$"** symbol on his lists to remind him of his true ability to afford the items.

Rasher Celebrates AIM and Aha Successes

Max, like all the rascals in the taming process, needs to keep a PAT (**P**ositive **A**ccomplishment **T**hankful) journal. As Max engages in new behaviors, he needs to record the positive aspects he is learning about.

The PAT journal, his personal PAT on the back, captures the new positive emotions, as well as the experience of controlling money in a new way. At times when Max may feel like it is all too difficult or slow moving, he can reread the entries from previous days and weeks to give him a dose of renewed encouragement.

Summary of Taming Strategies for Rasher

♦ Claim the old beliefs that have misguided you.
♦ Reconstruct them to create new, useful beliefs.
♦ Claim and tame any sneakers that have strayed into your rascal.
♦ Set up a regular time weekly to organize and pay bills.
♦ Look at your Pain/Gain ratios for insight and clarification.
♦ Visit the other fiscal rascals for tips and take AIM action.
♦ Make a list of low and no-cost alternatives to shopping that you enjoy.
♦ Pay attention to your progress and celebrate it.
♦ Leave a little space in the budget for the old Rasher's fun.
♦ When debt free, put your former debt payments into savings for long term and short term needs.
♦ Establish a financial plan to put your goals in perspective.

Clasher

*They call me **Clasher** 'cuz I fight mySELF,*
I can't decide if I want stuff or wealth!
I save my money for a while but then,
I take it ALL and find a way to spend!
No matter what I do, I feel a fool,
Like either way I'm breaking someone's rule!

Claiming Clasher

"Clashers" - urge to splurge one minute, then crave to save the next and consequently are known for sabotaging their own savings efforts, because one desire *clashes* with another equally strong one. Clashers are like recovering Rashers or Flashers, in the sense that they decide to get their spending under control, but every time they save up a sum of money, they get tempted by a desirable item, and they end up spending all or most of their money.

Clashers may have been raised by individuals with two opposing styles, a Casher and a Flasher, for example. By swinging back and forth between the two extremes, Clashers have difficulty finding and sticking with a healthy balance. No matter what Clashers do, they feel like they're betraying or disobeying one side.

Clashers have the nickname, "Hasher," because decisions about saving and spending may get postponed in order to "hash over" what to do. It's an impossible dilemma because the two conflicting styles can't seem to resolve their differences. This procrastination may go on for many years or even a lifetime. Clashers yearn to be rid of their ambivalence, yet the very nature of their "beast" keeps them unsettled and frustrated.

Case History: May Bea Clasher

Meet May Bea Clasher. In her future, she May Bea poor, she May Bea rich, or she May Bea somewhere in between. It depends on whether her indecision about how to handle her money is ever resolved.

At age 35, May has an extensive history of false starts with savings. When she first began working in her early twenties, her employer offered a retirement savings program. At an enrollment meeting for employees, May learned that she could save a percentage of her income and not pay tax on that amount. Plus, her employer would put in half of every dollar May saved. It made sense to May, so she eagerly began her participation in the plan. This was May's only savings, but it accumulated handsomely. May didn't know how much money she would need in retirement, but this seemed like a good start.

May changed employers four years later, receiving a job she was enthusiastic about even though her new employer didn't have a retirement plan. Now her retirement money from her previous employer seemed to jump out at her with flailing arms in an excited plea to buy some of the things she had done without in earlier years. That vacation in Hawaii, new furniture and car were among the items she wanted.

Clasher's urge to splurge

May had more than $15,000 in her retirement account and her friends all seemed to be having more fun than she was. Her yearning to be included in the fun grew, so one day she made an innocent call to find out how she could withdraw some of her money. She learned she could take *all* the money out if she wanted to. It would all be taxable and she would have to pay a 10% penalty for withdrawing the money before reaching age 59 1/2.

At first May thought, "Well, maybe I ought to just leave it alone." Later that day she began to think, "Maybe I'll take out just enough to go to Hawaii." But as she sat on her sofa pondering the dilemma, the sofa began to look older and older - uglier and uglier. By the end of the day, May had requested a complete distribution of her money, booked her trip to Hawaii and had gone furniture shopping.

Clasher's craving for saving

When May returned home from Hawaii, she plopped her new luggage and souvenirs on the floor. She plopped herself onto the new sofa she had purchased before leaving on her trip and thought, "*Maybe* I should go through my mail." The sheer quantity of bills in that pile gave May a new resolve to start saving money again and get her spending under control. "*Maybe* I'll start an IRA," she thought "Or *maybe* I should just pay off all these bills first. Or *maybe* I should just save some money in the bank. Or *maybe* I should do a little of both. Yes, that's it. Or *maybe*. . ."

A year later, May had paid down most of her debt but hadn't saved any money. She had just finished her tax returns and yikes! Because of the extra taxes and penalties for withdrawing her retirement account, she owed money to the IRS. Because she didn't have any emergency money saved, she took an advance on her credit card to pay the taxes.

This seemed quite discouraging to May. The best she could do was think, "*Maybe* I'll be able to save after I get these taxes paid off." But then she thought, "*Maybe* I should give up on saving. Or *maybe* I should do a little of both."

This time she did a little of both. She hated the taxes and penalties from using her retirement money prematurely, so she put none of her money in an IRA. She wanted to be able to access it easily and without such "harsh punishment" (as she thought of it) for using it.

The "emergency" fund

Though her savings grew much more slowly than her original retirement plan with her first employer, it was a nice emergency fund. The problem was, May could not determine what "qualified" as a true emergency.

Over the years she depleted, then rebuilt it several times because of "emergencies" such as a new wardrobe, a travel club and an upgrade to her home entertainment center. Her emergency fund looked like a roller coaster and she had never restarted any retirement savings, even though her current employer now offered a 401K plan.

It seemed like no matter what May did, she was restless about her money decisions. Over the years she sometimes shopped at discount stores, other times at very exclusive ones, other times she went without items she wanted for extended periods until she felt utterly deprived and went on a shopping spree.

Now in her mid-thirties, she could see she would soon have two decades of working under her belt and nothing much to show for it. At the last employee meeting, she learned she would need more money than she ever imagined in order to retire with anywhere near the income she was currently spending. May began thinking, "*Maybe* it's time to get into my employer's plan..." The power in May's Clasher personality left her emotionally unsettled, baffled, and perpetually insecure financially.

The May Bea Clasher profile

Now we'll look at Clasher's profile, starting with her BOB. Remember, Clasher may not be aware of this bundle of beliefs, which she developed over her lifetime. *Italicized* words represent the extremes, or rigid, subjective aspect of the belief. Next, we'll look at the four types of money handling habits (PETS) typical of a Clasher and a sample list of the COOL/FOOL rules she created from her interpretation of life's experiences.

Clasher's Invisible and Distorted Bundle of Beliefs
(Original BOB in extreme)

1. I should *always* buy the least expensive items.
2. I should *always* buy the most expensive items.
3. I should *save* my money.
4. I should *spend* my money.
5. I'll get my money figured out *later!*
6. I can't *ever win.*
7. I need to handle my money affairs *perfectly* or it's *no use.*
8. I'm *no good* with money and can't *ever* make up my mind.

Clasher's *Physical* Habits of Handling Money

- Buys things and then returns the items.
- Has unfinished or inconsistent record keeping.
- Saves some money, but inadequate amounts.
- Withdraws savings amounts for impulse buys.
- Has no plan or organized purpose to spending or saving.
- May read about investments and financial planning, but doesn't take consistent action.
- Uses credit cards excessively at times, cash only at other times (when trying to "reform").
- Procrastinates in making decisions.

Clasher's *Emotional* Habits With Money

Clashers experience a wide range of emotions with money, because they can swing from one extreme to another when it comes to spending and saving. Refer to Rasher and Flasher for the spending emotions and Casher and Stasher for the savings emotions. Otherwise, Clashers are generally experiencing some form of the following emotions about money:

Ambivalent	Disturbed
Anxious	Flustered
Confused	Guilty
Discontented	Lost
Disloyal	Uncertain
Restless	Unsettled

Clasher's *Thought* Habits With Money

- Thinks spending and saving are both important.
- Has difficulty deciding what, when, where and how to manage money.
- Wants to do what's right, but thinks there is no right answer about money.
- Sometimes thinks learning about money is interesting (high priority).
- Other times thinks learning about money is very dull . (low priority).

Clasher's *Social* Habits With Money

- Sometimes goes out with friends and spends freely.
- Other times declines invitations and isolates.
- Inconsistently buys gifts, sometimes lavish, at other times budget-oriented.
- Vulnerable to peer pressure and the perceived judgments of others.
- Spends more when with people than when alone.

COOL/FOOL Rules Clasher Mistakenly Created

- Finding bargains proves your self worth.
- Buy luxury items to affirm your self worth.
- Procrastinate about savings and financial record keeping.
- Don't commit to any financial decisions.
- Feel disloyal, ambivalent or conflicted no matter what you do with money.

Taming Clasher

(Author's note: The taming strategies for all rascals have a number of things in common. Before proceeding, be familiar with the strategies for change in the book's introduction, "Taming Your Fiscal Rascal.")

Clasher's conflicting urges have created problems for her. She can get fiscally fit by accepting her rascal and developing a plan that starts with reconstructing her BOB.

The Pain/Gain Ratio for May Bea Clasher

May has tried a variety of savings plans, in an effort to quiet her unsettled fiscal rascal. What she has in her favor is peace on the job front, so her income is stable. But that peaceful feeling is lost in her decision-making about how to manage her money.

When she originally enrolled in her company plan, May was pleased that she didn't miss the money being taken out of her check much, so her pain rating was a 5. On the other hand, May wasn't all that excited by the savings accumulation. Her gain rating was also a 5. With a 5/5 ratio, she had a PF (pain factor) of exactly 1. As long as nothing was changing . . . well, nothing was changing. The lure of satisfying her urge to splurge would eventually sabotage May's savings.

When May felt the peer pressure to go to Hawaii, it seemed to trigger her spending desires. This happened to coincide with her retirement account rolling over from her previous employer. Suddenly the money seemed more available than ever. Now, preserving her money had a pain rating of 8, with the perceived gain descending to a 2. With such a ratio (8/2 = 4 PF), May was highly likely to make a change, but it was a change that would damage her financial picture.

Her long term savings suffered at the hands of her short term desires.

This. . . or that. . . or these. . . or those. . .

The problem, as we have seen in May's case, is that she wasn't satisfied or at peace either way. Her first shift toward making a change again came when she created debt in order to pay the extra taxes brought on by cashing in her retirement fund. By the time her savings went up and down several more times (all the while paying off the stubborn debt), May's frustration had intensified.

Her *money* hadn't grown, but her *disharmony* had! She wanted to settle in and get more consistent in her feelings, thoughts and actions with money. Now May's pain rating from *not* saving was an 8 and her perception of gain from spending was a 4. This meant May's PF for having no savings became a 2. Her readiness for a positive change had increased.

Financial baggage is a good thing...to lose

May Bea Clasher was tired of being such a *maybe* about her fiscal matters. She was ready to rid herself of the ambivalence that had become so familiar to her. May prepared to begin quantifying her genuine financial needs and let *them* be the power that steered her money personality, instead of her conflicting unconscious urges.

May's heavy financial "baggage" had allowed her 'urge to splurge' to dominate over her 'craving for saving.' She was vulnerable to the constant exposure and societal reinforcements to spend. Although her Clasher rascal wanted both saving *and* spending, the spending messages frequented her more often than the savings messages, causing May to give in to the temptation to spend.

May needed to lose the Clasher financial baggage, so she could take back the power in her money personality to combat the problematic urge to splurge.

Reconstructing Clasher's Bundle of Beliefs

In reviewing the BOB lists for Clasher, May claimed a presence for all of them. The PI (presence intensity) was strongest for the beliefs, "I can't win with money" and "I'm no good with money and can't make up my mind." The first thing she wanted to work on was the defeatist attitude she had developed and to build up her confidence. But she also wanted to better understand why she had conflicting and opposing "shoulds" in her head. Spend or save? Frugal or regal? Now or later? High risk or low risk? Long term or short term?

Clasher's Bundle of Beliefs (Original BOB in extreme)	Clasher's Reconstructed Beliefs (New Goals)
1. I should always buy the least expensive items.	1. Sometimes the least expensive item is the best decision.
2. I should always buy the most expensive items.	2. Sometimes the most expensive item is the best decision.
3. I should save my money.	3. I save a reasonable amount of money based on my values, goals, and priorities.
4. I should spend my money.	4. I spend money based on my values, goals and priorities.
5. I'll get my money figured out later!	5. My overall financial plan helps me with both the present and the future.
6. I can't ever win.	6. I can win with my goals.
7. I must handle my money affairs perfectly or it's no use.	7. I handle my money affairs even if it's imperfect or not yet complete.
8. I'm no good with money and can't make up my mind.	8. I am fine with money and can make decisions adequately.

The Power in Your Money Personality

In some respects, we can all relate to May Bea Clasher. The choices and opportunities we have before us in our society are vast. As wonderful as that is, it is also confusing to the point of being overwhelming at times. May Bea Clasher is a classic back and forth, up and down, conflicted-sometimes-saver-sometimes-spender.

May has a history of saving. . . then spending her savings. In this respect, she seems to have gotten nowhere although she is at least aware of the importance of saving for long term needs such as retirement. May is also inconsistent in how she goes about making her plan choices. She confuses the plan with the investment choice and hasn't been able to connect her goals for the money with which choice she should make.

In this classic Clasher rascal case, May is considering participation in her employer's retirement plan. She seems to have a love/hate relationship with money. May loves, yet hates spending and loves, yet hates saving. She has experienced the sting of government penalties and taxes for taking money out of a plan prematurely, which has left her uncertain about ever setting money aside in such a plan. She is unclear about the "pretax" concept and how that helps her savings grow over time.

May grew up in a family in which her parents were almost exact opposites in money styles. Her mother was a free spirit who liked nice things and did a lot of shopping and spending. She pushed for a larger home. Her father stressed savings and frugality as a virtue. He was content in their average home. They fought about money, but the fights never seemed to end in resolution, they just stopped until the next one. May just craved peace and harmony.

> **They fought about money, but the fights never seemed to end in resolution, they just stopped until the next one.**

In applying the reconstructed beliefs, May found that with some changes in her information gathering, she could begin to trust in the new belief, *"I **can** win with money."*

She had operated with too little information to make high quality, appropriate financial decisions. May was able to forgive herself for her past results by recognizing that it was an *inadequacy* of information, **not** her personal inadequacy that lead to the discouraging outcome.

Help from a money planner

May decided she would meet with the financial planner who had been recommended to her and utilize the planner's services if she was willing and able to take the time to educate her in a patient and affirming way. May would interview more than one planner if she felt her educational and other needs would not be met by the first one. By identifying the criteria she wanted, May had confidence that the task was manageable.

This process helped her affirm and accept the related new belief, "I am fine with money and can make decisions adequately." May discovered that one of her own misguided beliefs in the Clasher style had been that she was inferior or incompetent if she needed help with her financial planning. May started talking to people she respected and asked if they used a financial planner. She was pleased to hear that she wasn't alone in her confusion. Many of her associates had sought advice from various financial consultants and their feedback was encouraging.

May also admitted to a strong presence of the belief that she would get her money figured out later. Not unlike getting a second scoop of ice cream and uttering, "I'll start my diet tomorrow," this kind of belief could lead to a lifetime of procrastination. May Bea looked at a chart showing that to reach a savings goal it takes about three times as much money for every decade of lost time. May found this motivating in helping her commit to a long term plan.

Clasher's AIM: Changing and Balancing Habits

May went through the list of habits for Clasher and found she could relate to many of them. The Physical habits list was especially striking to May. She had done every one of the items on the list and found it stimulating to rewrite the habits into opposite behaviors.

The Power in Your Money Personality

May had already identified record keeping as a problem area. She had saved money at times, but never knew what amount would be adequate. With a financial plan, she would now be able to more clearly define what "adequate" was, which would help level out her back-and-forth spending pattern.

As part of her improved habits, May decided that she would determine how much money she would allocate for gifts on a monthly basis. This category of social habits had bothered her and she felt a relief at having a more analytical way to approach the decision. She realized that by following her financial plan, she would have reason to be less impulsive and less vulnerable to peer pressure.

May was finding that when information was presented to her in a way she understood, it held her interest. May decided that she had tremendous reason to be interested in her present financial picture, because it would impact her future. One of her primary AIMs was to modify her interest and stop telling herself that learning about money is dull. She was going to make it a higher priority, which she realized would not take as much time as she had originally expected.

Emotional habits intriguing

May was intrigued by the list of emotional money habits for Clashers, partly because of the concept of emotions being habitual. She decided that indeed, she had established a habit of feeling the clasher emotions almost as though they were a permanent, established definition of herself. She went through the list and checked off each emotion, then changed them to new emotional goals for how she felt about money. She recognized the link between the thoughts and feelings and had already experienced some change in her emotions, just by clarifying her goals and scheduling a financial plan meeting. Emotional habits that were already changing included:

ambivalent	*to*	*determined*
anxious	*to*	*confident*
confused	*to*	*learning*
discontented	*to*	*contented*
lost	*to*	*focused*
uncertain	*to*	*goal directed*

May found the word "disloyal" to ring true when she saw it on the list, but she couldn't put her finger on what that was about. In working through the personal money history questionnaire found in the couples chapter, however, May began to see that her exposure to two very different money styles was at the root of her feeling of disloyalty.

Simply stated, when May spent money, she felt like she was honoring her mother's values, but that meant she was being disloyal to her father's. When she saved money, the opposite feeling emerged. Either way, she felt disloyal because of her parents' opposite and unresolved style differences. This also explained May's uneasy feeling of guilt that seemed to hover over her financial affairs.

May's uncertainty, along with many of her other restless feelings stemmed from the disharmony between her mother and father. The absence of effective communication about financial matters in her developmental years left her with no other possible conclusion about money than the last word on Clasher's emotional habits list - "unsettled."

> **The absence of effective communication about financial matters in her developmental years left her with no other possible conclusion about money than the last word on Clasher's emotional habits list - "unsettled."**

Was it any wonder that May Bea procrastinated and was inconsistent in her own decision making about money? With no consistent or reliable guide, she was floundering, and floundering became her impression of normal.

Clasher Visiting Other Rascals

May needed to pay a visit to all of the rascals, because they all had elements she could relate to. Since her inconsistency leaned more to a default of spending, she needed to focus on the positive habits of Casher and Stasher to find greater balance. This would fit well with her new resolve to put a financial plan in place.

Action Honoring Awareness (Aha!) Ideas

Enroll in the plan: The first action May should take to honor her new awareness (Aha!) is to enroll in her employer's 401K plan. She found out her dollars would be matched 50% for every dollar she saved up to 6%. At first, she didn't understand this formula. But then she remembered her reconstructed belief, "I am fine with money and can make decisions adequately." She asked again for clarification and this time she understood. The 6% figure represented a percentage of her pay. It was confusing again at first glance, but May persevered and took a second look at the examples in the enrollment kit.

Understand the plan: May now understood she could defer (save) up to 15% of her salary (payroll) into the plan. Her employer would put in 50 cents for every dollar she saved up to 6% of the 15% allowed. It simply meant that for the dollars she saved *over* 6% of her salary, there was no match 50 cent match.

Did that mean she should only save 6% because the rest of the dollars didn't get a match? No. Every dollar she saved reduced her taxable income, so even though she didn't get the match (she liked to call it free money), she did get money saved and lowered taxes.

May didn't have debt and heavy interest charges to be concerned about, so she had no reason to decline full participation in the plan. She had already lost several years of time and this could help get her back on track. Plus, once she enrolled, the saving was automatic and didn't require her to do anything, other than review and update her investment allocations as needed.

Organize bills: May also lacked an organized bill paying system, so she was going to use the "Monthly Bills Ledger" (see Appendix). She also would prepare a spending plan after she met with her financial planner.

May wanted to see how much she should be saving so her goals could be achieved within the time frame she wanted. That would take some number crunching from her planner. Once she knew how much to set aside for savings each month, she could allocate the remainder into a guilt-free spending plan.

Journal it: May was directed to the journal idea for Flasher and Rasher. She would do those exercises for a few weeks to make sure her spending habits and any related emotional challenges were attended to while making these changes.

Clasher Celebrates AIM and Aha Successes

May had good reason to be proud of her efforts. No more *"maybe"* for May Bea! She was taking many positive steps and thriving on the progress. May would keep her PAT (**P**ositive **A**ccomplishment **T**hankful) journal and write down all of the steps she was taking. One of her accomplishments was persistency in seeking information so that she understood the answers she was getting. It had taken courage on her part when she asked for clarification on the 401K plan's matching program. But it was an important lesson to learn that she was competent and able to grasp these financial subjects. May gave herself a pat on the back for her new financial sensibility.

Summary of Taming Strategies for Clasher

- ◆ Claim the old beliefs that have misguided you.
- ◆ Reconstruct them to create new, useful beliefs.
- ◆ Claim and tame any sneakers that have strayed into your rascal.
- ◆ Set aside regular and consistent time to organize your financial affairs.
- ◆ Use the Pain/Gain ratios to reinforce changes.
- ◆ Visit the other rascals for tips and try opposing behaviors (AIM).
- ◆ Enroll in your 401K plan and save the maximum amount allowed.
- ◆ Hire a financial planner to help with your savings goals.
- ◆ Persist in getting clear information.
- ◆ Record and celebrate progress and successes.

Rascal #4

Dasher

*My name is **Dasher** and I'm in a rush,*
If you say "plan" to me I'll tell you, "Hush!"
I'm in a hurry, no time to worry--
My thought of money is a little blurry!
I've got to go now, don't you dare say "No" now,
When I am ready, I will just say "Whoa now!"

Claiming Dasher

"Dashers" - are too busy to notice if they have an urge to splurge or a craving for saving. They **dash** around, always rushing from one activity to another - all except money activities, that is. Dashers aren't so consumed with the thrill of spending (like flashers and rashers), but instead simply don't get around to planning and organizing their money. This may be due to a feeling of disinterest, boredom, confusion, or incompetence about it.

Dashers value their busy-ness but often feel overextended. They may not even balance their checkbooks or know how much income is incoming. Dashers have one thing in common with Clashers - they may avoid money activities in the belief that they will "hash over" what to do later but they manage to be too busy to get to it. Dashers want to avoid boredom, but the price they pay for that financially is often severe, due to never getting around to setting aside money for their future.

Case History: Dan D. Dasher

Meet Dan D. Dasher. He feels *dandy* about the many ways he keeps busy with life's activities. It gives him a sense of purpose and meaning. He has stuck with his original job, because he's been too busy to think about making a change. Besides, he gets time off in the summer and his pay raises are automatic and reliable, which keeps it simple.

Dan coaches little league in the summer and paints houses for extra income. He takes a vacation with his family. He teaches community education classes on home fix-it projects every Tuesday. He has several projects "in the works" on his own home. He is program director in the local Chamber of Commerce. He and his wife are in the PTA and try to play racquet ball at least twice a week.

The snowball effect

It seems as though each activity Dan is involved in invites the opportunity to participate in several others. Dan has a difficult time saying no to these invitations. By the time he is actually home, the last thing he wants to think about is financial matters. Dan knows the bills need to be paid, so he occasionally retrieves the envelopes from the mail pile that look like bills, writes a few checks and hastily stashes the receipts in another pile. Sometimes he forgets to mail them, other times he remembers to mail them but forgets to put postage on them. If the check register is handy, that's dandy - he records the checks he writes. However, if it isn't handy, he doesn't record the checks. When a bill says his last payment wasn't received, he assumes that must be correct, (it takes too much time to try to look it up) so he pays double - only to find out in the next bill that he's overpaid. Dan's record keeping is **not** handy and there is nothing dandy about it.

Every now and then, Dan happens to see a quick news story on financial planning. A flurry of large figures *dash* by and perhaps an idea or two. Dan thinks, "Well that's just *dandy* - how does anyone get that done?" He tells himself he'll look into it next week. Dan has no idea how much money he will need later in life and it hasn't even occurred to him that it's a question he should ask himself. Even if the question jumped into Dan's path, he wouldn't know where to go for the answer, so the wonder is fleeting at best.

Dan sometimes wonders how much household spending is in certain categories. This pops up at times when his attention is momentarily focused on items like his son's new baseball shoes. Dan is amazed at the brands and prices. "Why do kids have to have stuff like this these days?" he questions himself. "I wonder how much we spend on the kids clothes in a year. And what amount for shoes alone?" But there isn't time to linger on that thought - they've got a game to get to. Dan utters a quick gripe, shrugs and is off to the game.

Dan is getting ready for a PTA meeting one evening and the phone rings. His father has had a massive heart attack and is in intensive care. When Dan arrives at the Intensive Care Unit, he is stunned by the sounds, smells and sight of his father hooked up to all the monitors. His father opens his eyes and wearily says, "The doctors say I have to slow down." But sadly, for Dan's father, it's too late. After a monumental struggle, Dan's father passes away.

The power in Dan's Dasher money personality had paved the way to financial procrastination and neglect. For Dan, it was this major loss of his father that motivated him to find a healthier balance.

The Dan D. Dasher Profile

We examine Dasher's profile by first reviewing his BOB, the bundle of beliefs Dan accumulated over his busy life. *Italicized* words represent the extremes or subjective part of the belief. Then we'll look at the four types of money handling habits (PETS) associated with Dasher, and the COOL/FOOL rules of behavior he came to expect of himself.

Dasher's Invisible and Distorted Bundle of Beliefs
(Original BOB in extreme)

1. I *never* have time to deal with my money.
2. Planning and organizing my money life would be *impossible* and overwhelming.
3. I am better off avoiding *all* my *money matters.*
4. *Everything* else I do is more important than my money management.
5. My money issues will *take care of themselves.*
6. Keeping money records takes *too long* and is a waste of time.
7. I shouldn't bother to manage my money unless I do it thoroughly and *perfectly.*
8. If I have to seek financial advice, I'm a *loser.*

Dasher's *Physical* Habits of Handling Money

- Organization is usually lacking, even chaotic.
- Rarely plans time to pay bills and review savings.
- Bills may get paid too late or even too early because of busy-ness.
- May have errors in record keeping due to rushed handling.
- Shops in a rush, so usually no time to research the best prices.
- May make overly quick decisions resulting in impulse purchases.
- Savings are either non-existent or neglected, and under diversified.

Dasher's *Emotional* Habits With Money

- Anxious (but usually not intensely or often)
- Apathetic, ambivalent
- Indifferent, distracted
- Irritated, pressured
- Restless, unsettled
- Scattered

Dasher's *Thought* Habits With Money

- Has good intentions for savings, but usually runs out of time or energy for it.
- Thinks savings is a terrific idea, but gets terrifically bored researching it.
- Makes, then breaks promises to self to get it done next week, next month, next year, etc.
- Wonders how other people actually get it done.
- Doesn't think about the cost of procrastination in savings.
- Tries not to think about it.

Dasher's *Social* Habits With Money

- May tend to "go with the crowd" to keep it simple and quick.
- Prefers speedy decisions, so may take charge of ideas if group appears wishy-washy.
- Decisions tend not to be based on seeking status or prestige.
- Usually fairly pragmatic with social spending.
- Pays fair share of expenses, treats others in turn.

COOL/FOOL Rules Dasher Mistakenly Created

- Avoid money management, but never seek advice.
- Pretend money matters will take care of themselves.
- When feeling uncomfortable about ignoring money, try to ignore that, too.

Taming Dasher

(Author's note: The taming strategies for all rascals have a number of things in common. Before proceeding, I would remind the reader to be familiar with the introduction "Taming Your Fiscal Rascals.")

In the case of Dan D. Dasher, some of the taming strategies are similar to Clasher. One of the key differences, however, is Dasher hasn't felt much, if any, emotional turmoil about money decisions. Whereas Clasher has expended considerable energy feeling unsettled and switching back and forth from saving to spending, Dasher has never given it much thought or emotional energy either way. Dan D. prefers to believe it's just *dandy* having a full, occupied life.

The frantic, busy lives many of us lead these days, causes many little things to be left undone. It's a "to do" list that is impossibly long: doing the family's laundry, car repairs, house cleaning, changing the light bulbs, trips to the doctor, dentist, orthodontist, keeping in touch with family, church activities, the mail, hair cuts, grocery shopping, walking the dog, vacations, weddings, funerals, fixing the leaky faucet, putting gas in the car, birthdays, holidays, kids' sports, school, piano lessons, mowing the lawn or shoveling the snow - oh, and there are those full time jobs that both mom and dad are heroically holding down. Now let's see - have we left anything off the list?

We have, indeed, left something off the list - money management. Minding, tending, planning, or whatever we prefer to call it, falls off the "to do" list. As important and necessary as money is in our life, *it* doesn't nag us for attention.

If only money could talk . . .

The dog whines for a walk. Hair grows so we get it cut. The church calls for our participation. Hunger won't let us neglect groceries. Mother gets upset if we don't call or write. We run out of clothes if we don't do the laundry. But money just sits there. . . silently.

> **But money just sits there...silently. Money doesn't complain if we part with it too soon.**

Money never says, "I think we need to talk about our relationship." It doesn't complain if we part with it too soon. It will not question where we send it, or why. Our money doesn't scream at us when we put it in the wrong place. It never sobs in grief when we forget all about it. If it did, we would hear deafening screams of protest throughout our neighborhoods, shopping centers, casinos, car dealerships, etc. Some of the money we are parting with would be screaming out in horror.

The "*dollar holler*" might exclaim utterances such as:

- *"Hey! I'm supposed to go to the electric company."*
- *"Wait just a darn minute! You said you'd send me to your IRA."*
- *"Forget it! I'm scheduled for the rent payment."*
- *"What the. . . ? Get me out of here! I belong in your savings account."*
- *"Now stop right there! I refuse to be traded for another beanie baby."*
- *"Put me back in your wallet this minute. I just got here, for Pete's sake!"*
- *"Not again! You promised you'd keep me out of slot machines forever."*

For a rascal like Dasher, or *any* of the money rascals for that matter, it's too bad we can't teach money to speak up and cry out. Dan is pretty good at taking directions, especially if they are loud enough to get his attention. In some respects, that is how Dan D. Dasher will get tamed. Let's have a look.

The Pain/Gain Ratio for Dan D. Dasher

We've all gotta love Dan D. Dasher just a little bit. His overextended schedule is something with which we can all relate on some level. His motives are good. His motto might sound a little like that of Forrest Gump's mother. "Life is like a gas tank. Fill 'er up!"

As we have seen in the case of Dan D. Dasher, there wasn't much that could slow him down - that's why his name sounds like a race horse. He would only occasionally think about money as something to be planful about. Before his father died, if Dan had been asked to rate the pain of being so busy compared to the gain, he would have blurted out, "1/10!" as he rushed by. The fact that his busy-ness caused him to neglect his financial planning was not a concern. With a PF (pain factor) of only .1, Dan D's motivation to change couldn't be any smaller.

The loss of a loved one, especially prematurely (Dan's father was only 59), can suddenly bring new clarity to what was once a thick fog. Many values come into question. There is a financial component that usually makes its way through the side door, if it hasn't already come crashing through the front door. For Dan, it was the latter.

When funeral arrangements were being made, Dan's mother told him she had no idea what she was going to do financially. Dan's father had been a busy man. He hadn't managed to put much aside for retirement and the only life insurance he had was the group policy that was part of his employee benefit package. Now, with the same Pain/Gain question posed to Dan, he had a dramatically different answer.

The grief was so profound and his father's style so similar to his own. The inescapable implication was that his father's frantic pace had somehow contributed to his death. Now Dan's pain rating had completely reversed. There is no gain if you lose your life in the process. Dan's dashing had come to a screeching halt. His pain factor was a 10 (10/1) and he vowed to slow down. The multitude of sudden and acute questions would change the way Dan approached his activities forever more.

Reconstructing Dasher's Bundle of Beliefs

Dan recognized himself in his review of the invisible BOB list, with his highest "presence intensity" (PI) score of 10 landing on beliefs number 4, 5, and 6 of the eight listed:

Dasher's Bundle of Beliefs (Original BOB in extreme)	Dasher's Reconstructed Beliefs (New Goals)
1. I don't have time to deal with my money.	1. I find enough time to deal with my money.
2. Planning and organizing my money life would be impossible and overwhelming.	2. I am able to competently organize my money life.
3. I am better off avoiding my money matters.	3. Avoiding money matters now costs me a lot of money in the future.
4. Everything else I do is more important than my money management.	4. Money management is as important as other things I do.
5. My money issues will take care of themselves.	5. Taking care of my money issues is up to me.
6. Keeping money records takes too long and is a waste of time.	6. Keeping basic money records is valuable and saves me time overall.
7. I shouldn't bother to manage my money unless I do it thoroughly and perfectly.	7. I will keep adequate records that capture the information I need.
8. If I seek financial advice, I'm a loser.	8. I am a winner for seeking financial advice when there are so many options to consider.

Now Dan could see two of the direct consequences of being over-extended and over-scheduled. If the rush reached "hyper" activity, health consequences became real as he was now seeing with his father. If money matters were consistently neglected, important actions never got taken, leaving some severe voids in the event of sudden loss, such as death.

Dan could see the inaccuracy of the first belief and he embraced the reconstructed version of it, "Money management is as important as other things I do." Dan added, "In fact, it is *more* important than some of the stuff I *have* been doing. I'd probably be better off teaching one less community education class and getting my bills in order. I'd probably make more in saved interest charges than I do teaching the class. I don't enjoy it like I used to, anyway."

This was a significant shift for Dan. He hadn't taken the time before to even think about whether he enjoyed what he *was* doing with his time. He asked himself, "Am I really running *to* things, or am I perhaps running *away* from something?"

Money doesn't talk

It was clear, too, that money issues did not "take care of themselves," as reflected in the second belief Dan claimed. Yes, money did flow in and out of his checking account and his pockets, but it didn't sign itself up for life insurance or a retirement plan.

Dan could now see this in living color in the worried face of his mother. Her reality served as a mirror reflection of the financial vulnerability Dan's own family faced. Dan had a special fondness for the "dollar holler" vision and decided to use that metaphor to help him target his own goals. His favorite picture of the protesting dollar was the one that reflected his hurried style in everything, including the fast outflow of money.

> **Yes, money did flow in and out of his checking account and his pockets, but it didn't sign itself up for life insurance or a retirement plan.**

Dan decided to visualize that talking money hollering out to him (nicknamed **"Dollar Holler"**):

> *"Put me back in your wallet this minute. I just got here, for Pete's sake!"*

The Dollar Holler became a game that he could visualize when starting to organize his budget and to allocate expenses in a more planful and prioritized way.

As we have seen with the other fiscal rascals, Dan immediately related to some of the invisible beliefs and some he initially rejected until he thought about them more. For example, at first he rejected the related beliefs, "Keeping money records takes too long and is a waste of time" and "Planning and organizing my money life would be impossible and overwhelming." But when asked how much time he thought that would take, he figured it would be at least twelve hours a week. "I don't have that kind of time!" he exclaimed.

His first inaccuracy in this case was his estimated time expenditure. He could use the basic monthly bill paying system which would only take about two hours a week. It would be a world of improvement over his non-systematic way of paying bills and it wouldn't involve the tedious detail he'd imagined.

Dan admitted that in the back of his mind, he believed *"organization = overwhelming."* But this was due to his definition of organization as covering every single possible detail.

The reconstructed belief allowed for a less than perfect system to create a much needed organization. In reality, a little bit of organization gained him time instead of costing him time. Imagine that.

Dasher's AIM: Changing and Balancing Habits

Organize bills: Dan went through the list of habits for Dasher. He decided to Act **A**s **I**f **M**odified on the organizational money front first. He planned to set aside Wednesday evenings from 6:30-8:00. He would record any new bills that had arrived in the mail onto his "Monthly Bills Ledger" (see Appendix) and pay any bills coming due before the next Wednesday. By recording the balances and amounts paid each month, Dan had a good picture of the progress being made, as well as a quick reference he could use for any discrepancies that might occur. This prevented overpaying and the occasional extra charges that had plagued Dan, due to his erratic payments in the past.

One of the physical habits Dan began to change was handling daily mail, especially bills. Dan established shelf space for three kinds of mail: "junk," "bills" and "other." The bills were opened daily and put in his bill paying folder. On Wednesdays, he recorded the balances and amounts due with the due date on the monthly ledger.

The envelopes for mailing had the payment slip inside, with the due date and minimum amount due written on the envelope where the stamp would go. The envelopes were stored chronologically by due date, with the earlier dates due at the top. Any additional receipts were filed in an accordion file by month. Dan also paid any bills coming due on Wednesdays and recorded the amount and date he sent the payment. To make it more obvious to him when he had finished paying a specific bill, Dan highlighted the amount in yellow.

Dan now was discovering first hand that organization didn't have to occupy mountains of time. In fact, what had occupied more time in the earlier disorganized days, was mountains of paper. Dan found that he also could give himself a visual pat on the back on his ledger by circling or highlighting balances that were on their way down - like his credit card debt. Dan was more conscious about his spending now that he had a composite of the total debt. It helped him reevaluate some of his spending now that he could see how quickly it piled up.

Slow down: The primary social habit that Dan decided to pay more attention to was the central theme of his lifestyle. Often he spent money in a rush without thinking about whether he genuinely valued what it got him. He decided to slow down and be a little more independent in his social decisions, which meant sometimes not going along with the crowd.

Dan D. was getting more handy with his money now and taking pride in his changed mental habits. Now that his record keeping was established and in a maintenance mode, he could start to plan his savings and investments.

His emotional habits were now in line with a more relaxed, yet controlled method of "tending his tender." Dan had amended his apathy, ambivalence, pressure and restlessness to being interested, decisive, calm and settled. These relatively minor changes gave Dan a sense of wellness that spread beyond his money matters and into other areas of his life. He was surprised at this unexpected benefit.

> **His emotional habits were now in line with a more relaxed, yet controlled method of "tending his tender."**

Dasher Visiting Other Rascals

Dan visited the savings rascals, Casher and Stasher, to give him some habits to expand his list of new goals. He was eager to create greater balance in his life and add some simplicity. He had been void of any conscious craving for saving and was ready to build up some saving muscle. By looking at the Basher rascals' goals of modesty and frugal styles, he gathered some thoughts on making his money handling more values-based.

Action Honoring Awareness (Aha!) Ideas

Financial analysis: As Dan did not have any immediate financial crisis to undo, most of his strategies were organizational, as discussed in the previous section. The additional steps Dan took included starting a long term retirement savings account and having a life insurance analysis done for his family. He also found a financial planner that would work with his mother as well as he and his wife.

Medical analysis: Dan had a medical check up to put his mind at ease about his own health. His physician assured him that he was in good health, but encouraged him to begin a regular exercise program to improve his aerobic fitness for its long term benefits. Dan's dashing was no replacement for exercise! In fact, his doctor insisted, *less* dashing and more walking was vital to Dan for health maintenance.

Dasher Celebrates AIM and Aha Successes

Dan found that his favorite place to record his successes was on his "Monthly Bills Ledger" (see Appendix). For now, he noted his PATs (**P**ositive/**A**ccomplishment/**T**hankful) on the back of the ledger sheet each Wednesday. If he got feelings of discouragement, he would reread the PATs and add others, including ones not related to money. He found that sometimes, the less he felt like doing it, the more beneficial it was.

Summary of Taming Strategies for Dasher

♦ Claim the old beliefs that have misguided you.
♦ Reconstruct them to create new, useful beliefs.
♦ Claim and tame any sneakers that have strayed into your rascal.
♦ Set aside time to organize your financial affairs.
♦ Use the Pain/Gain exercises to review needed change.
♦ Visit the other rascals for tips and try opposing behaviors (AIM).
♦ Begin bill paying and record keeping once a week.
♦ Meet with a financial planner to help match savings plans with goals.
♦ Celebrate and record progress for encouragement.

Basher

*My name is **Basher** and I think wealth's bad,*
The chase for money really makes me mad.
The less I have the more I feel all right,
I keep life modest so I'll see the light.
To keep my money feels just plain greedy,
I'd rather give it to folks who are needy.

Claiming Basher

"Bashers" - **bash** wealth, and may be critical or suspicious of people who like money and the luxuries it can provide, believing it may "breed greed," evil or selfishness. Bashers probably invented the expression, "filthy rich." They reject any urge to splurge or craving for saving as selfish. Bashers may fear being criticized for wealth, so they make sure to be virtuous by living a modest lifestyle.

Bashers are the opposite of Flashers in the sense that they attempt to display their virtue by *not* buying luxuries. Bashers tend to earn smaller incomes and may feel guilty if they keep or earn too much money. They often choose the helping professions or work for non-profit organizations.

Bashers may give money away or find other ways of making it disappear if they start to feel they have too much. Bashers feel uneasy talking about money and do not want to think of making profits with it. Consequently, they may be uncomfortable investing it.

Case History: Leslie Basher

Meet Leslie Basher (everybody calls her Les). Her motto is, "*Less* is more." Les is extremely troubled by the materialism of her society. She consciously chooses to keep life simple and modest. She was once offered a job where her income would have nearly doubled. She was afraid, however, that this would spoil her.

Les wants *less* material goods, *less* income, *less* money accumulated and *less* greed and evil in the world. The *less* Les buys, the more virtuous she feels. The *less* she has, the more honorable she feels. The more she gives to charity, the *less* selfish she feels. The lingering fear for Les, is that if she ever compromises these strict values, she will be "selling out" on her convictions and will spiral into an evil, out-of-control lifestyle.

Les works in a non-profit social service agency. Her income is modest, which suits her quite well and as long as she stays in her small efficiency apartment she can make ends meet. She is a little unsettled by the crime in her neighborhood, however, and occasionally finds herself wishing she could afford to move out. She promptly feels guilty at such a thought and banishes it from her mind. Besides, this is where more help is needed, so "I should offer it without hesitation. I need to put others first," she reminds herself.

Les is careful with her shopping and searches garage sales, the Goodwill and Salvation Army stores for basic household items such as dishes, rugs and towels. Often she can find adequate clothing there as well. Being thrifty is the only way Les can have any money to donate to her church and favorite charities.

Not all of her coworkers feel quite as strongly as she does about modest living. In some ways, it appears to Les that they are enjoying life more than she is. So when Penny Pincher and Marta Martyr invited her to go to a dinner theater with them one Friday night, she agreed. Once there, however, Les was excited yet uncomfortable. This pleasure might be overdoing it. Les ordered the least expensive dinner on the menu even though she could afford more. She felt a little less guilty spending the least amount possible and getting something less attractive to her.

While at the play she observed the audience members around her. Their appearance seemed crisp, fresh, new and lavish. "These people must spend more on one outfit than I do on my whole wardrobe," she thought. At this she felt a certain pride. Even Penny and Marta looked a little overdone to Les. Les knew she would have to decline any such future invitations. She didn't want to "catch" this greed disease.

Les had ignored her savings for many years and had recently begun thinking it would be acceptable to save modestly for retirement. She wouldn't need much, but "nothing" would probably be too little, even for Les. When she heard mutual fund advertising that used words like "wealth, aggressive growth, performance and portfolio diversification" she felt suspicious and mismatched. The returns she heard about seemed too mysterious and too big for her.

Les opened a money market IRA at the bank and planned to add $50 a month into it. This, she *guessed,* would provide her with a modest income in her retirement years and it was simpler to understand than the other investments she'd heard about.

The Les Basher Profile

The Basher profile starts with the BOB and moves on through the four different kinds of money handling habits and COOL/FOOL rules. Remember, the *italicized* words in the BOB list emphasize the distorted part of the belief, or terms that are subject to many varying definitions. Let's take a look.

Basher's Invisible and Distorted Bundle of Beliefs
(Original BOB in extreme)

1. *Rich* people are *selfish* and not nice.
2. I am *nice*, therefore I better not be rich!
3. Wealth causes people to be hung up on money and *nothing* else.
4. It is *sinful* to have a lot of money.
5. If I earn *a lot* of money, I should give it to charitable causes.
6. Living *modestly* is the only way to stay focused on important human values.
7. You have to hurt other people in order to create *wealth*.
8. If I save my money, I am being selfish and *greedy*.

Basher's *Physical* Habits of Handling Money

- Maintains modest lifestyle.
- Buys used material goods, including clothes, whenever possible.
- Spends as little as possible and will search for low prices.
- Invests conservatively.
- May contribute substantial amounts to charities or church.
- Tracks spending to monitor thriftiness and allocate amounts to worthy causes.

Basher's *Emotional* Habits With Money

- Guilty (if earns, keeps, or spends too much money on self)
- Superior (to those with wealth)

- Righteous
- Confused, disturbed (by others' "obsession" with money)
- Peaceful, contented (when living modestly)
- Suspicious, distrustful (of others' motives)
- Disappointed (by others' greed)
- Apathetic (about investing or growing money)

Basher's *Thought* Habits With Money

- Wealth causes selfishness or greediness.
- May negatively and harshly judge others with money.
- Spending on self for things beyond basic necessities is wrong.
- Getting well paid for work you enjoy is wrong.
- Using money for pleasure is wrong.
- Giving to others is *always* right.
- Money is the root of *all* evil.

Basher's *Social* Habits With Money

- Spends more on other causes than on personal lifestyle.
- Prefers low budget activities.
- Declines invitations that are perceived to be too self-indulgent or lavish.
- Financial decisions based on potential societal benefit.
- Works in lower paying, community service jobs.
- Loans money for worthy causes.
- Helping others is highest priority.

COOL/FOOL Rules Basher Mistakenly Created

- Avoid becoming *wealthy* in order to *assure virtue.*
- Giving money *generously* to charitable causes means I am worthwhile.
- *Always* put others' financial needs ahead of my own.
- Reject any *large* income and savings to prove goodness.
- Live very *modestly* to avoid becoming spoiled.

Taming Basher

(Author's note: The taming strategies for all rascals have a number of things in common. Before proceeding, I would direct the reader to look at the introduction - "Taming Your Fiscal Rascals.")

Les Basher, like other Bashers, is guided by her strong conviction that money is bad. The mistaken logic that follows for a person who wants to be good, is that if money is bad and I have money, then I am bad. The better, or "gooder" people strive to be, the *less* money they believe they should have. Thus, *less* is more. Like any good idea, the problem is born out of overdoing a good thing and the subjectivity of determining how modest is modest enough is a difficult call.

One of the objectives of using the money rascal styles is to create awareness of distortions in one's thought patterns. This subjective discovery needs to be made by each individual. It cannot be forced or imposed upon any person, because the motivation for change must come from within.

An important measure of whether one has gotten too much of a good thing, can be in searching more deeply into one's motives for the ceaseless increase of a certain trait. When overemphasizing money in either direction, the error is in attempting to achieve a type of superiority over others by pursuing the trait to an extreme.

> **When overemphasizing money in either direction, the error is in attempting to achieve a type of superiority over others by pursuing the trait to an extreme.**

When one starts to feel cheated or martyr-like, that can serve as an alert to having crossed the line away from the original goal and into a different territory. When rascals go too far, it can be helpful to search for this kind of phenomenon in seeking solutions. Emotions can be a useful tool for "busting" a belief. Sometimes they are almost like ghosts that haunt us. Yet emotions are actually indicators of underlying belief systems that have created expectations that may not be realistic. They can help us become our own financial ghost busters.

A good model for some

In some respects, what Les and other Bashers are trying to accomplish is a good model for others who really do get carried away in their spending behaviors. The Flashers of the world make the Bashers all the more committed to their charter, because of the extreme extravagance of their flashy material strivings.

The taming guide for Les Basher and the other rascals uses emotional well being of the individual as the primary indicator of whether a problem has developed. Where to draw the line as to how much is enough or how much is too much is a deeply personal matter. The self report of the individual's feeling of harmony, happiness or contentment is used as a measure of whether the person has overdone his or her own pursuits.

In the case of Les, she has begun to feel uneasy in her choices, even though she fights her own senses and seems to be sticking with a more austere existence than she is genuinely comfortable with. When the definition of being good begins to require a certain misery in order to feel successful, that can serve as a red flag for easing up on the criteria. This is the exploratory process Les Basher would go through in "fiscal therapy."

The Pain/Gain Ratio for Les Basher

It appears that Les has begun to question where she needs to draw the line to stay within her convictions. Some of her self-sacrificing behaviors have begun to take a modest toll on her peace of mind. This is something she feels she should no longer dismiss.

The fact that Les felt superior to others who were living modestly but not as modestly as she was, indicated a distortion of her original purpose. Her original purpose was to be generous, good, and serve human welfare. But by comparing her efforts to those of others and judging them as inferior, the purity of her original Basher intent had become tainted.

Les felt unsafe where she lived, yet had denied her feelings on this topic. Although there wasn't a specific triggering event to cause a shift in her feelings of serenity, she described a weariness that left her feeling a sense of disturbing apathy. Les felt *less* energetic in everything she did. When she first noticed her body aches and feeling of heaviness, she thought she had the flu. But it wasn't going away.

> # Les felt unsafe where she lived, yet had denied her feelings on this topic.

Before these symptoms appeared, Les would have said the pain of her meager lifestyle was non-existent. She hesitatingly gave it a rating of 2, after arguing with herself about whether zero was the real rating. What she got out of living this way, she reported, was an 8 (gain). With a PF (pain factor) score so far below 1 (2/8 = .25), the likelihood of Les changing her lifestyle was extremely low.

After some months of this heavy, achy feeling, however, Les began reconsidering these questions. Her self-denial was breaking down and she reassessed her Pain/Gain ratio twice in a three month period. First Les moved her Pain/Gain to 4/4 (= 1, or neutral for motivation to change), and the third time she rated it 6/3 (PF now a 2).

These shifts came when Les was asked to say more about her feelings during different decision points in her life. When she turned down a better paying job, for example, she felt a certain honor and strength in her convictions. Les recognized, however, that she also had "tinges" of feeling uneasy, sad, even cheated. On her evening at the dinner theater, she felt deprived and left out.

With her PF moving to greater than 1, a readiness for change was indicated. In discussing her wages and lifestyle in more depth, Les felt encouraged when reminded that it wasn't an all or nothing proposition. She didn't have to chose the "double or nothing" route. She could, however, move up a notch or two in her wages and still fall within her criteria for goodness. A small difference might make a large difference for Les.

With her motivation to change growing in this way, Les was ready to examine the Basher bundle of beliefs. Taming her rascal would bring some welcome relief and rebalance her money personality power.

Reconstructing Basher's Bundle of Beliefs

Les gave the Basher list of invisible beliefs a thorough going over and began to adjust how she defined some fiscal matters.

Basher's Bundle of Beliefs (Original BOB in extreme)	Basher's Reconstructed Beliefs (New Goals)
1. Rich people are selfish and not nice.	1. Generosity and kindness is about individual choice, not wealth.
2. I am nice, therefore I better not be rich!	2. I am nice by choice, whether wealthy or not!
3. Wealth causes people to be hung up on money and nothing else.	3. I am in control of my values regardless of my financial position.
4. It is sinful to have a lot of money.	4. Sinfulness is related to behavior, not the presence or absence of wealth.
5. If I earn a lot of money, I should give it to charitable causes.	5. If I earn a lot of money, there are many diverse ways to put it to good use.
6. Living modestly is the only way to stay focused on important human values.	6. I live according to my values, no matter how much money I have.
7. You have to hurt other people in order to create wealth.	7. The creation of wealth helps many people, and contributes to much growth.
8. If I save my money, I am being selfish and greedy.	8. Saving my money assures that I will not be a burden to others in the future.

One of the first realizations the list created for Les, was that she had never really defined what *selfishness* or *greed* meant. These, and similar words, popped up in several of the beliefs and Les did think these extremes had been part of her bundle. Les knew the words generated an emotional response in her every time she heard them. She felt repulsed, and this seemed extreme to Les.

Les began to work on having a clearer meaning and understanding of the words, rather than simply continuing on her path of trying to make sure she *wasn't* greedy, selfish, sinful or hurtful.

In her effort to *avoid* being greedy or selfish, Les realized, she had mistakenly defined non-selfishness as requiring her to be totally self*less*. Les began to see there was a vast middle ground that she had never bothered to explore before.

> **In her effort to *avoid* being greedy or selfish, Les realized, she had mistakenly defined non-selfishness as requiring her to be totally self*less*.**

In her exploration of this topic, Les found stories of self-sacrifice that resulted in overall *greater harm than good*. An important concept for Les was the idea that the practice of being overly selfless could cause one to become a burden to others as a result of giving beyond one's true capacity.

Sacrificing too much can be viewed as an indulgence that creates as many, or more problems than it solves. Les felt a sting of recognition in these ideas and was intent on reaching a healthier perspective on the choices she had been making.

In reviewing the themes of the misguided Basher beliefs, Les found that she had unknowingly attached significant attributes and meanings to money itself. The reconstructions of the beliefs were important to her in separating money from human attributes. Generosity and kindness are about individual choice, not wealth. Wealth is not the cause of sinfulness or hurtfulness. By separating money from values, Les could see more clearly that the mere possession of wealth was not in and of itself, good or bad, right or wrong.

Basher's AIM: Changing and Balancing Habits

Clarify terms: The habits of the Basher group of rascals were helpful to Les as she began to clarify her criteria for staying within her values. She could see that in many respects, she had simply tried to outdo herself in virtuous living. She went through the lists and picked out every word that needed further definition, so that she could begin to assign at least some degree of quantification to it.

Les had been vague about her idea of what "modest," meant, for example, in terms of lifestyle. She was rigid and strict in her attempt to live modestly, however. Other words she would begin to define more clearly included: "little, low, conservative, substantial, thriftiness, self-indulgent, lavish, and worthy."

She found that she had often assigned an all-or-nothing thought pattern to these words. "Whenever possible. . ." had become "always" to Les, so if she ever bought anything that was new instead of used, she felt ashamed. "Spend little," in her own mind had really become "spend nothing." Although spending nothing was literally impossible, that had become her ideal.

This left Les feeling guilty or unsuccessful every time she spent money on anything. This no-win dilemma was a major contributor to her current weariness. Armed with clearer definitions, her aches began to diminish and her energy returned.

Give to self: These clarifications helped Les, first by giving her back some freedom to include herself on the list of "beneficiaries of money." She decided to change the physical habit, "Buys used material goods, including clothes, whenever possible" to "*Sometimes* buys used goods rather than new." By moving "sometimes" to the front of the sentence, it reminded Les that she was not morally bound to buying used goods 100% of the time. One of her new personal AIMs (Act **A**s **I**f **M**odified), was to buy a new item every month, and buy one new item of clothing with each seasonal change.

Instead of declining all invitations that seemed lavish, she would take a day to ponder it rather than automatically rejecting it. This gave her the time to use her new lists and reflect on more than one criteria for ruling it in or out.

Accept pleasure: Les also decided to Act **A**s **I**f **M**odified in her rejection of pleasure. One of the mental habits she found she wanted to reconstruct was, "Using money for pleasure is wrong." She modified it to: "I may use money for pleasure and still be a good person." Her new AIM was to do something pleasurable at least once a month.

Basher Visiting Other Rascals

Les cautiously peered at the habits of Flasher and Rasher to find a couple of ways she might treat herself for a change. From Flasher she borrowed the idea of eating at a fine restaurant. From Rasher she borrowed the idea of buying something impulsively. Both of these ideas were going to be acted on infrequently. No one would suggest going so far as to turn a Basher into an impulsive and frequent shopper. But by allowing a pinch of excitement and spontaneity into her life, Les could free herself up from some of her former self-imposed prison of "no exceptions allowed" discipline. Les also looked at the savers to begin assessing changes she could make there.

Action Honoring Awareness (Aha!) Ideas

Review career options: Some of the actions Les planned to take are discussed in the AIM section. Les was also going to begin to look at other jobs she was qualified for. Now that she had a new awareness of how strictly she had kept her definition of "modest and low" where money was concerned, she felt she could permit herself to investigate a better job. Instead of the old motto, "Less is more," Les changed it to, "Less is less!" Her networking activities and ongoing career research were rejuvenating to her.

Plan pleasure: Les adjusted her budget to allow a larger percentage of her income to be used for a pleasurable activity or new item each month. Les also started to pay attention to other things she could begin to allow herself to do. She started a file where she would save ideas in the form of brochures and advertisements and refer to it when it was time for her to do something for pleasure.

Support system: Les also took action by talking to a friend about the discoveries she was experiencing, so that she could continue to get another perspective on the issues. Some of the questions were still difficult to answer in a quantitative manner, and these discussions helped Les expand her thinking and make decisions in a new way.

Basher Celebrates AIM and Aha Successes

Les maintained her PAT journal with great discipline, of course. One of the things she included as an accomplishment was "fun." She made a note when she did fun things or felt excited about something and congratulated herself on remembering to put herself on the "Who to do good deeds for" list. She also recorded other things that still honored her original convictions, so that she could remain true to them as well.

Summary of Taming Strategies for Basher

◆ Claim the old beliefs that have misguided you.
◆ Reconstruct them to create new, useful beliefs.
◆ Claim and tame any sneakers that have strayed into your rascal.
◆ Begin including yourself on the list of recipients of your good deeds.
◆ Look at your Pain/Gain ratios for insight and clarification.
◆ Visit the other fiscal rascals for tips and take AIM and Aha actions.
◆ Keep a list of pleasurable or fun activities you can do occasionally.
◆ Keep your definitions in the gray area instead of black or white.
◆ Record your positive progress and celebrate it.
◆ Begin saving for yourself so that you do not become someone's burden in the future.
◆ Match your goals with a financial plan.

Rascal #6

Asher

*My name is **Asher** 'cuz I'm ashen and pale,*
My money worries make me feel so frail.
Whether there's a lot or only just a little,
What I should do is such a freaky riddle!
So leave me be now, or I'll get upset,
It just seems money always makes me fret!

Claiming Asher

"Ashers" - crave to save their way out of their financial worries. They are burned out, **ashen** and pale in color from fretting so much about money. Ashers feel helpless and fear many aspects of money management, including earning enough of it to feel secure.

Extreme Ashers may be skeptical of any growth at all and therefore, keep cash "hidden" in places like the cookie jar or under the mattress rather than trust a financial institution or advisor with it.

Usually Ashers are reluctant to spend and may be married to spenders, which feeds the fear. Ashers are the most fearful and discontent of the rascals and may be neglectful out of anxiety over what to do with money, fearing that if they make the wrong choice it will ALL disappear. An untamed and dominant Asher rascal can easily end up feeling worn out, isolated and bitter from a lifetime of championship worrying.

Case History: Cary A. Burden

Meet Cary Asher Burden. What is this burden being *carried* by Asher you ask? Is it all about fret? You bet! Cary Asher has logged olympic championship hours of tension, fretting over money issues and gnashing his teeth. Alas, this is why his friends have several aliases for him, including Gnasher Asher and Despairy Cary.

Asher frets about debts whether he has any or not. Just the mere *thought* of having debt is enough to increase the weight of the burden Cary must carry. The weight of all the fretting logged by Cary A. Burden is downright heroic. Is it any wonder that he sometimes ends up as a little pile of burned out *ashes?*

Cary Asher resembles both Casher and Basher in his reluctance to spend money. But the *reason* for his thriftiness is different than either of them. Whereas Basher underspends to be honorable and pure, Cary does so out of fear that his money will run out.

While Casher likes to save money in liquid, cash accounts for control and predictability, Cary hangs on to it out of an exaggerated feeling of incompetence at managing it any other way. This low self confidence is another burden carried by Cary Asher.

Cary's underlying low self-esteem is a problem on several fronts. He wants to earn as much as possible, but he does not feel deserving of it. His self-doubt prevents him from being a top wage earner, but his income goal does help him muster the courage to seek better paying work. However, when he does achieve the job promotions and raises he has sought, he feels like a fraud.

Cary wonders when his employer will discover the truth of how incompetent he really is. His true underlying feeling of unworthiness increases his anxiety that it's all going to suddenly vanish one day. This worry over what might go wrong in the future creates a vicious cycle of never-ending insecurity and poor Cary never seems to have anything to celebrate and feel good about.

When Cary is invited on social outings, he attends if it's free and he's been notified enough in advance. He declines otherwise. He is horrified if someone asks him for a loan. The reason or purpose of the loan is irrelevant as far as Cary is concerned. The answer, of course, is "no" - but he hates the feeling of confrontation it generates. To most other requests he's an extremely agreeable, helpful person. He will part with his time to help others, but he will *not* part with his money.

After many years, Asher is likely to have accumulated many dollars, but he has no joyful, spontaneous memories to look back on and he is beginning to wonder why he still worries. He wants to feel better and stop being Gnasher Asher, but he has no idea where to begin.

The power in Cary's Asher money personality keeps him a victim of his own worries and stifles his spending to extremes. It also creates distance in his primary relationships, especially his marriage. Both spouses feel left out when one carries such deep worry burdens.

The Cary A. (Asher) Burden Profile

Asher's profile includes his BOB, the four types of money handling habits (PETS), and some of the COOL/FOOL rules he created for himself. *Italicized* words in the lists are reminders of the extreme or subjective part of the belief. We'll examine them more closely.

Asher's Invisible Bundle of Beliefs
(Original BOB in extreme)

1. There is *never enough* money.
2. I am *always incompetent* with money.
3. Money is more *powerful* than I am.
4. *All* of my money is going to vanish if I'm not *careful*.
5. Others can't be trusted with my *money matters*.
6. I am not *good enough* to make *a lot* of money.
7. Money is overwhelming and should *always* be *worried* about.
8. It's not *safe* to spend money, because I might need it later.

Asher's *Physical* Habits of Handling Money

- May save excessive amounts for countless "rainy days" feared coming in the future.
- Savings are conservative and accessible.
- Keeps accurate records for "security checks" on safety and amounts in case of need.
- Work chosen for predictable, dependable paycheck.
- Pays bills on time or early.
- Avoids using credit cards and other debt.
- May be partnered with spender, creating severe conflict with preferences.
- Shops for needed items only, and looks for lowest prices.

Asher's *Emotional* Habits With Money

- Anxious and worried (about everything)
- Burdened, weary (from trying to control all outcomes)
- Fearful, uptight, tense
- Distraught, despairing (at how impossible it feels)
- Insecure, uneasy (from not knowing what the future holds)
- Incapable, incompetent
- Overwhelmed (by responsibility)
- Cheated (if inadequate money or others spending)
- Sad, depressed
- Responsible, justified (in worry)
- Pressured (to control future)
- Vulnerable (to things not in control)
- Weepy (when unexpected expenses arise)

Asher's *Thought* Habits With Money

- Believes unnecessary spending will cause shortages later.
- Worries about unexpected expenses that may come up.
- Hates irresponsible spending decisions.
- Wants control and predictability with money.
- Being planful is the way to be responsible.
- Thinks spontaneity is irresponsible.
- Should always reflect about spending before doing it.
- Saving is better and more enjoyable than spending.

Asher's *Social* Habits With Money

- Never "treats" when out socially.
- Pays only his exact share of expense.
- Prefers fast-food or cafeteria restaurants (poor tipper!).
- Avoids pleasure spending, declines costly invitations.
- Looks for "freebies."
- Never loans money.

COOL/FOOL Rules Asher Mistakenly Created

- Keep perfect records to make sure no money gets lost.
- Worry about money all the time.
- Never use an advisor for money matters.
- Always save money instead of spending it.

Taming Asher

(Author's note: The taming strategies for all rascals have a number of things in common. Before proceeding, make sure you are familiar with the strategies for change in the introduction - "Taming Your Fiscal Rascals.")

Cary A. (Asher) Burden is a chronic worrier. Money frightens Cary because of his inability to totally control what happens with it. Cary has been extremely cautious (very cary-ful!) in decisions throughout his life. When his first job paid a modest salary, Cary was afraid of unexpected expenses that he couldn't afford, such as car repairs. He had built up savings over the years, so that now if the car needed repair, it wouldn't be a problem.

At one point Cary had enough to buy a whole new car if he had to, but then he worried that some other catastrophe might cause financial ruin. He once was notified that he was chosen for a routine tax audit and he felt panicked. Before he even realized where his thoughts were headed, he had begun visualizing the auditor with a grim look on his face saying, "You've got a problem here." In his catastrophic vision of these events, he saw gigantic penalties which wiped him out financially. He tried to tell his wife about his fears and he was startled by his own tears. He heard himself wailing, "What are we going to do? We'll be ruined. I can't handle this."

The Pain/Gain Ratio for Cary A. Burden (Asher)

Cary had difficulty pinpointing if there had been a specific incident that had heightened his tension over money issues. At first glance, he could find nothing out of the ordinary that had been happening. Everything at his job was normal. He and his wife, Mary, were empty nesters. Their three grown children were doing well and their youngest child, Carrie, had graduated from college two years earlier. Cary and Mary were thrilled to have the college bills behind them.

Their middle child Barry, had decided to attend graduate school, but was not asking his parents to pay for it. The master's degree, he said, would be costly in the short run, but should give him a worthwhile boost in pay later on. His current employer would allow him to cut his weekly work hours in order to do the class work. The extra time would help him get his studies taken care of, but not his bills. His pay would decrease proportionately to the decrease in hours. Barry would utilize some school loans to help make up the difference.

Life was moving positively along its way. In fact, their oldest son, Harry, had just announced that he and his wife, Sherry, were expecting a baby.

Cary had passed through many life stages while struggling along with his money anxieties. But he had managed to systematically save quite a sum of money over the years. He made the maximum contribution to his 401K plan, as did Mary. He kept the money in conservative investment choices and moved it around every time he heard the market was going to correct, even though only 20% of his total money was in stock mutual funds.

Cary had always worked hard to keep the family living within its means and by his estimates, they should be okay for retirement. His worrying ways were a drain on him, but only about a 5 on the pain scale. "Besides,they keep me focused on doing the right thing," Cary claimed. That benefit of doing the "right thing" gave his gain rating a score of 8. With a 5/8 Pain/Gain ratio, his PF was under 1 (.62). In Cary's view, there wasn't much reason to change at this point.

Shortly after learning that Barry was going back to school and Harry's wife was expecting a baby, Cary began to worry about *their* financial affairs. He felt like he should help Barry out, but he couldn't afford it. But, Cary worried, what if Barry spends all his money on this degree and it doesn't bring the pay increase he was banking on? He also felt like he and Mary should do something special financially for the baby, but then, they felt, they would have to do the same thing for all the future grandchildren and that might be too great a burden.

Cary now realized these seemingly positive life events were bringing on more worry for him. This added burden to his already hefty daily dose of anxieties had raised his pain rating from 5 to 9. Because his actions (keeping his money) weren't matching his feelings about what he ought to be doing (sharing his money), Cary saw the gain rating go down to a 3. This new 9/3 ratio brought his pain factor up to a 3, which provided ample motivation to make a change.

Reconstructing Asher's Bundle of Beliefs

Asher's Bundle of Beliefs (Original BOB in extreme)	Asher's Reconstructed Beliefs (New Goals)
1. There is never enough money.	1. I have many resources to make sure I have enough money.
2. I am incompetent with money.	2. I am competent with money.
3. Money is more powerful than I am.	3. It is up to me to keep my power, rather than to give it away mistakenly.
4. All of my money is going to vanish if I'm not careful.	4. I am able to manage my finances well and keep it well balanced and secure.
5. Others can't be trusted with my money matters.	5. There are many trustworthy financial advisors and I trust myself to choose one.
6. I am not good enough to make a lot of money.	6. I am good enough to make the money I need.
7. Money is overwhelming and should be worried about.	7. I can learn what I need to know to take care of my money and stop worrying.
8. It's not safe to spend money, because I might need it later.	8. My financial plan helps me see what I can spend and still keep my future secure.

118

Cary, in his hope to find relief from his burden of worries, went through the bundle of beliefs for Asher. At first Cary checked off every belief on the list. When he went back over each one to assign a "presence intensity" score, he scored the following items the highest:

- *There is never enough money. (10)*
- *All of my money is going to vanish if I'm not careful. (10)*
- *It's not safe to spend money, because I might need it later. (9)*
- *Others can't be trusted with my money matters. (8)*

Cary thought back on his money life and found that no matter how much extra money they had at different times, he'd always had the feeling that there wasn't enough. When asked whether there had *actually* been enough, Cary carefully scanned his memory. He knew his books. He knew his records. Cary's reply was, "Yes."

Hearing himself answer this question in the affirmative sent an unidentified surge through his body. It wasn't exactly a painful feeling, but it was strange.

Cary's counselor asked, *"Can you describe the feeling more?"*

Cary answered, *"It's fast, and flowing, and cool - or is it hot? I can't tell, but it goes from my stomach up through my chest and settles in my head."*

"And what does your head want to say when it gets there?" asked the counselor.

Cary uttered simply, *"Wow."*

"What does 'wow' tell you?" his counselor persisted.

Dumbstruck, Cary revealed, *"It tells me I've had enough money all along. Oh, my gosh!"*

"Even when Mary wasn't working and you had three young children at home?" the counselor asked.

"Yes. Things were tight, but we were okay.

"Even after you bought the bigger house?"

"Yes."

"What about the time you took out a loan to help pay tuition a few years ago?"

"Yes." A deep and welcome sense of relief came over Cary.

The reconstructed belief for "There is never enough money" was, "I have many resources to make sure I have enough money." Cary confessed that he hadn't genuinely believed the reconstructed belief when he first read it. His initial reaction was to defend his original belief. But now Cary was seeing the reality - there had been enough money all along. His worries had become a bad habit.

Cary's original error was imagining how catastrophic it would be if all the money vanished. It was as though the first two beliefs in the bundle were strung together with a "because" word. "There is never enough money *because* all of my money is going to vanish" (if I'm not careful). When you have a fear that it's all going to disappear, of course there can never be enough. Cary could now see how this previously invisible fear had misdirected many of his money actions and fretful reactions.

Cary agreed with the reconstructed belief, "I am able to manage my finances well and keep them well balanced and secure." He felt inspired by the saying, "Worry is a misuse of the imagination."

Cary also added other reconstructions because he felt he needed to counter his irrational fear that all his money might disappear. He modified it to state simply, "My money is adequate and preserved for any unexpected needs." This relieved him of the all-or-nothing component of the old belief (*all* my money might vanish). Plus, it erased the burden of responsibility from him (if *I'm* not careful). The old belief had shackled him into the role of being overly responsible for everything remotely related to money, making him a warrior doing battle with the forces that would vaporize his money if he weren't careful.

Cary's additional reconstruction was, "There is always enough money." Cary's fear of the opposite was so deeply ingrained that he felt he needed a more strongly stated reconstruction of the old belief. Cary said, "If my *'never'* mentality dukes it out with my *'always'* mentality, I'll probably end up somewhere in between - and I think that's a big improvement."

> # The old belief had shackled him into the role of being overly responsible for everything remotely related to money...

Rascal uniqueness

This is an excellent example of the uniqueness of each person's fiscal rascals. Think of how dangerous it would be to emphasize Cary's new belief to Flasher, the flashy spender. If Flasher went around reminding himself over and over, "There is always enough money," instead of a spending *rascal*, we would end up with a spending *monster*. But for Cary, the new belief brought him back to an overall balance. This new balance was essential as a tool to lighten Cary's *burdensome* load (remember his last name).

Now that Cary had gained some comfort with the idea that he had been overly careful and overly responsible for everything that might happen, he could see and understand more of his own sub-beliefs within the primary ones. In looking at the belief, "Others can't be trusted with my money matters," Cary saw multiple perfectionistic expectations about his money matters. He wanted it to grow, but never fluctuate, which was an impossible expectation. He wanted his money to be sheltered from taxes, but he didn't want penalties if he took it out before age 59 1/2. And with his old underlying belief that it was all going to vanish, Cary had carefully steered clear of all financial advisors, for fear that *they* might be the wicked force that would cause his money to disappear.

Asher's AIM: Changing and Balancing Habits

As we have seen with all of the fiscal rascals, Asher's habits match up with the BOB. The belief, "It is not safe to spend money because I might need it later," explains the first physical habit we see on Asher's list. Saving *excessive* amounts of money for countless "rainy days" of the future was one of Cary's habits.

Cary checked off any of the other habits he felt he had and looked for extremes within them. For example, he chose the physical habit, "Pays bills on time or early." Cary reported that he thought he probably "went overboard" in his handling of bills. He said he felt bothered by every bill that came in the mail. He felt like he couldn't get rid of them fast enough. His habit was to open every bill, every day. He would immediately write the checks to pay each bill, regardless of the due dates. If he really had his way, he would make a special trip to the post office and mail them, too.

When asked what he imagined happening if he did *not* pay his bills immediately, Cary was stumped at first. But when he was encouraged to close his eyes and picture it in his imagination, he got some clues. Cary said, "I can see the bills getting misplaced or lost. Then no one pays them, because they've disappeared. Then a second notice comes and I've gotten hit with a late charge. If I don't pay it right away, the process occurs all over again. Then bill collectors start calling my house - my credit is ruined - the money I needed to pay the bills has gone elsewhere, and I don't have enough to take care of it. It's a big mess."

What we might call Cary's chronic earliness in his bill paying habit, demonstrates his exaggerated fear of losing control. It all ties back to Asher's extreme underlying beliefs and Cary has decided to take AIM (Acting **As If M**odified) at his bill paying behavior. Now that he has been able to visualize the extremity of the underlying fear, he feels he can muster the courage to modify that behavior.

Adjust bill paying: He will delay his bill paying to fit the due date. Cary establishes a place to keep the bills (he still opens them daily), but waits to pay them until about a week before they are due. He will write checks for bills no more than once a week instead of daily as he is doing now. He is easing into this new behavior to minimize anxiety brought on by change. Notice he still allows plenty of time for the mail to deliver his payment, but at least he is no longer paying the bills several weeks early.

Cary can "modify his modification" later on as well. He may decide to stop opening his bills every day and open them just once a week at the time that he pays them. If once a week feels too infrequent to Cary, he can adjust and do it twice a week. He can also adjust when he mails the bills, based on where they are going.

There are many benefits to Cary from this one minor change. First, he confirms through experience that the bills do not get out of control using this more relaxed method. He's better able to enjoy his time after work, rather than always paying bills first. By keeping his money in his checking account longer, he earns more interest. Though it isn't earning a fortune by any stretch, the money adds up. From his house payment alone, Cary was losing $21 in interest each month by making the payment earlier than necessary. He estimated that waiting to pay his other bills until their due dates would preserve $10. For a rascal who doesn't want money to disappear, this strategy made sense.

My treat: One of the social habits that Cary decided to AIM at was, "Never treats when out socially." Cary modified that to, "Occasionally treats when out socially." Though he had difficulty determining how often "occasionally" was, Cary decided he would start by trying once a month. After three months, he could adjust his AIM to treat more or less frequently. The other criteria he added was that "treating" had to mean spending $10-20.

This idea reminded Cary that he can make up his own new rules, try them out and change in either direction as he goes along. The purpose is to learn some new habits, assess how well they're working and make adjustments when necessary. That's how Cary finds a new balance of his craving for saving.

From these changes, Cary will also learn to expand his thoughts and emotions inventory. His habits in these categories have been limited and narrow in their scope. Spontaneity and spending can be added to his inventory of thought habits. His emotional balance sheet can begin to accumulate more positive feelings as he learns to free up his restricted behaviors.

Inventory positive emotions: It is important for Cary to inventory the positive side of emotions that he discovers as he does his AIM behaviors. In treating his friend to dinner, for example, he rediscovered the feelings of delight and generosity. And just like paying off a debt, these new feelings eased some of the painful emotions that had become so habitual. Occasional treating had helped remove Cary's frequency of feeling fearful, uptight and tense. His emotional balance sheet was moving more toward gratifying and worry free "balance."

Asher Visiting Other Rascals

Cary had traits that were similar to Basher, although the underlying beliefs were different. But because they both have difficulty spending money, Cary decided to visit the spenders' habits to "shop" for ideas he could try on for size. Again, the goal is to help Cary find contained versions of the other rascals' behaviors to practice, not to abandon his useful traits in favor of an opposite extreme. He also looked at Dasher to find ideas of other activities in which he could engage to expand his constricted experiences.

Action Honoring Awareness (Aha!) Ideas

Disprove catastrophes: Cary came up with several ideas in doing the AIM exercises. In his awareness of his tendency for fears to escalate to an exaggerated extreme, he decided to repeatedly remind himself of the bad things that did *not* happen. For example, in paying his bills with the new method, he wanted to make sure the fear of losing control was continually *disproven*.

One way he did this was by repeating to himself, "See? Everything is fine. They aren't penalizing me for paying my bill later than I used to." He did this each time he opened the next month's bills. This reinforced the new behavior of waiting until the due date and "slaying the dragon" of fear that his bills would get out of control if he didn't pay them immediately. In a sense, it was like slaying the dragon over and over again until it was down for good.

Rejection of perfection: Another idea suggested to Cary was to purposely pay a bill imperfectly. He would select a bill to pay past the due date to reinforce the reality that lateness was not a pure catastrophe. This one experience could be "slipped into his hip pocket" as a reminder that nothing terrible happened from one slip up. That would help protect Cary from becoming overly rigid about any single method of bill paying. If he happened to have a schedule conflict on his bill paying night, for example, he would be less likely to feel anxious over missing it. He would reschedule his own bill paying meeting and avoid an emotional domino effect that begins with one change creating a chain of events eventually leading to catastrophe.

Entertainment plans: Cary also decided to take action that would begin to give him experiences that expanded the positive side of emotions. He was quite familiar with worry, pressure, and insecurity. He wanted to take action that would give him periods of relaxation and joy. He and Mary decided to go to a movie or play once a week. He chuckled at the awareness of enjoying being "the audience" because it was someone else's responsibility to entertain him. He got to be the "under-responsible" one by just sitting back and watching.

In earlier years, Cary had rarely enjoyed movies and plays because he hated to spend the money. Now that he has dispelled the fear that his money will *all* go away, he can relax more and not get so hung up on the expense aspect of the entertainment.

Money for grandchild: Cary also decided to get an education IRA for his grandchild. He would wait until the baby was born to take this action. He decided that he could afford to do that as a minimum for all of his grandchildren. He could also add more if he decided to do so later on.

Enjoy the present: This action honored his awareness that he did not have to have a plan for every single thing in the future. Yet it allowed him the pleasure of doing something for his grandchild, which had been his wish from the first time he heard the news. Now he could part with the money without fearing a giant siphon had just stolen away a vast portion of his money (the old vanishing dollars fear). Cary was aware that much of this was about enjoying the present at least as much as he had been worrying about the future.

Worst case worry paradox: Cary also decided to have a "worry" meeting once a week, until his habits had been modified enough to eliminate the need. He would have this session for half an hour the night after he had paid his bills. Any old anxieties that came up in the week needed to be postponed to fuss over at his worry meeting.

At his worry meeting Cary had to come up with as many fears as he could remember and list them on a piece of paper. Then he was to pick one or more fears and imagine the worst possible case with each one. This purposeful catastrophizing brought Cary back to more realistic expectations and paradoxically, even got him to chuckle at the funny side of the blown up exaggerations.

Investment advice: The other action Cary took to honor his awareness, was to seek some professional advice about his retirement projections and asset allocation. He now suspected that his choices had been overly conservative.

Adjust projections: In his projections of what his money would grow to by the time he and Mary retired, he had been using a very modest average rate of return of 4%. He began to think that this too, was an overly pessimistic assumption. What if he actually averaged 8%? This one number alone, made a profound difference in calculating the ultimate growth of his money. When he compromised and did the calculation using 6% instead of 4%, he discovered that his future dollars would be considerably greater than he had anticipated.

Reevaluate time horizon: If his calculations were correct, Cary would be better off than he originally thought in retirement. He was now looking to get another opinion on these questions, so he could reevaluate his old time assumptions. This gave him new hope and seemed to lift part of the heavy burden Cary was carrying.

Stop over-responsible self-pressuring: On the question of helping Barry with graduate school, Cary decided to take no action other than to stop worrying about him. Barry was an adult, capable of managing his financial affairs. For now, Cary was breaking his habit of over-responsible thoughts and actions. This was financial baggage he was relieved to lose. He would revisit the issue in six months to see if he wanted to change his decision in any way.

Asher Celebrates AIM and Aha Successes

Cary was keeping a journal of new habits and recognizing the ways they helped his emotional inventory achieve a better balance. He and Mary made a point of talking every evening about their PATs (Positive/Accomplishment/Thankfulness). Each week when they went to a movie or a play, they shared what had been the best part of the week for them. They also brainstormed on what additional activities they might enjoy and kept a list to draw from in their retirement years.

Summary of Taming Strategies for Asher

- ◆ Claim the old beliefs that have misguided you.
- ◆ Reconstruct them to create new, useful beliefs.
- ◆ Claim and tame any sneakers that have strayed into your rascal.
- ◆ Look at your Pain/Gain ratios for insight and clarification.
- ◆ Visit other fiscal rascals for tips and make AIM and Aha modifications.
- ◆ Postpone fiscal worries to your worry meeting once a week.
- ◆ Continue to reinforce "slaying the fear dragon" by disproving fears regularly.
- ◆ Treat others and share your money occasionally.
- ◆ Review your asset allocation and projections annually with the help of an investment advisor.
- ◆ Remember that you can adjust your changes as you go along.
- ◆ Keep looking for the positive emotions found in new and modified habits.

Casher

*Hello, I'm **Casher** and I'm in control,*
No cash of mine gets lost in a black hole!
I track it, black it, I may even stack it,
If it's not safe I don't think I could hack it!
I save my money if I have my druthers,
And leave the risk-taking to all the others!

Claiming Casher

"Cashers" - naturally crave to save and are the characters who like to "squirrel away" **cash** money and keep it safe for the future. Cashers are serious goal-setting/getting savers who like to keep track of their money, prioritize it, control it, budget it and perhaps do just about anything with it. . . except spend it! Others may think of them as tightwads because of their ultra discipline with spending.

Cashers rarely have an urge to splurge but if they do, they have no trouble resisting it. Money is security and control to Cashers. Cashers fear risk with money, so they prefer cautious, slow and steady growth. Cashers may have trouble trusting others with money and difficulty spending it on pleasure or nice items.

Case History: Stanley Casher

Meet the greatest number cruncher of the buncher - Casher. This rascal has no fear when it comes to doing math and working with figures. In fact, it is one of Casher's greatest satisfactions in life. Casher is such a natural at doing calculations that he insists on doing his own tax returns. Casher may not be much fun at the race track (you would never find him there - never, ever), but when it comes to tracking money, he reigns supreme. Casher wants control, discipline and predictability with his money above all. To accomplish that, a sound budget and tracking system is absolutely essential.

Stan Casher is never in a crunch financially because he has been so careful to plan his work and work his plan. His wife, Jan, calls him "Stan the Plan Man." Stan is so confident in his organizational systems, that when she teases Stan the Plan Man, he quips back, "Stan the Plan Man Can!" (Jan has artfully learned to tolerate his slightly overbearing organizational extreme, even if she has to get sneaky at times. But that's another story - watch for it in the next book in the Fiscal Rascal Series, *The Fiscal Rascals Get Married*, Chapter 7: "Jan Foils Stan the Plan Man." For a sneak preview in this book, go to "Fiscal Rascals in Relationships.")

Even as a kid, Stan remembers handling his money carefully. He still recalls the first time he was ever given a $5 bill. It was just before he left for camp. It seemed like a fortune. He wanted it to last. He didn't want to ever be without money again. When he went to camp with his fortune, he was not moved to buy the stuff the camp was selling. He hated to break the bill and preferred keeping his money rather than trading it for the things on display. After all, he reasoned, he might find something later that he liked better. He still remembers the feeling of triumph when he returned home, with money preserved for whatever the future might hold.

Stan took accounting classes in college and figured working with numbers would be the most useful way he could earn a living. He knew he wanted a secure and reliable job, one that he could count on. He eagerly applied the lessons he learned in business accounting to his own personal bookkeeping. Stan planned his spending and stuck with his sensible plan. He thought impulse buying was foolish and irresponsible. He organized all the bills chronologically by due date and kept a ledger for each month's expenses. He entered all of the household expenses into his financial software program and sorted them by category monthly. If they exceeded the budgeted amount, he made adjustments during the following month.

Stan also prepared for retirement. As with all of his savings, retirement money was put in interest bearing accounts, so that the principal would never go down. Stan liked doing projections of the retirement money and he wanted the long term calculations to be reliable.

The problem with his trusty interest rates however, was that they had steadily declined over the last decade, so that Stan's compounding projections were no longer accurate. The double digit interest rates he experienced in the eighties seemed to be gone forever. At this rate he had to save larger and larger portions of his earnings in order for his savings to adequately grow and provide the income Stan needed in his

The problem with his trusty interest rates, however, was that they had steadily declined over the last decade...

retirement years. At 12% interest, Stan estimated, his savings would double every six years. Yet at a 6% interest it would take 12 years to double his savings.

Stan was growing increasingly frustrated with the declining interest rates and for the first time ever, he considered venturing into some kind of managed funds. When Jan's employer began to offer a 401K plan, he looked more closely at the variety of investment choices and studied their historical performance. Stan wondered if this would be a good time to get into such risky choices.

The power in Stan's Casher rascal had confined him to very narrow choices, squelching his enjoyment of spending and eliminating any possibility of higher returns on his savings.

The Stan Casher Profile

We begin Casher's profile by looking at his BOB. Then we'll examine the four kinds of money handling habits (PETS) and a sample of COOL/FOOL rules which are typical of Cashers. Note the *italicized* words in the list that are extreme, rigid, or in need of definition.

Casher's Invisible Bundle of Beliefs
(Original BOB in extreme)

1. Responsible *people* carefully monitor *all* of their money flows to get it *right*.
2. I should keep *all* of my money in guaranteed interest accounts so it can't go down.
3. You never know when an emergency need will arise, so savings should *always* be top priority.
4. If I don't track every penny, my finances are *out of control*.
5. It is wasteful and totally foolish to buy things other than *necessities*.
6. Taking *any risk* with my money means it could all go away.
7. Life is serious business, and it's *wrong* to use money for enjoyment.
8. I should take care of *all* my financial management without *any* help.

Casher's *Physical* Habits of Handling Money

- Highly organized and disciplined.
- Pays bills on time.
- Knows balance sheet, budget and expenses.
- Pays with cash or checks, *not* credit cards.
- Savings are conservative, but plentiful.
- Stays debt free.
- May have a financial planner.

Casher's *Emotional* Habits With Money

- Worried, uncomfortable (if not saving or if any debt exists)
- Determined, enthused (to save for future)
- Satisfied (if saving adequately)
- Anxious (if savings aren't low risk)
- Superior (to spenders)
- Inspired (by compound interest!)
- Flustered (if someone else interferes in financial affairs)

Casher's *Thought* Habits With Money

- Debt is irresponsible and foolish.
- Savings is more important than spending.
- Spending beyond basic needs is unnecessary and boring.
- Satisfied with "status quo" (keep lifestyle reasonable).
- Savings should guarantee principal.
- Getting the best interest rates is the goal.
- Control and accuracy of money flow is the priority.

Casher's *Social* Habits With Money

- Will treat if his turn is overdue.
- Gives conservative, low cost gifts.
- Prefers separate checks in restaurants, for control.
- Minimal fun, pleasurable or extravagant spending.
- Planful rather than playful.
- Seldom willing to loan money.

COOL/FOOL Rules Casher Mistakenly Created

- Keep track of *every* dollar.
- Save *all* of my money in guaranteed interest accounts.
- Stay *perfectly in control* with my finances.
- Don't use *any* money for *unnecessary* things or for pure enjoyment.
- Do *all* of the money management functions myself.

Taming Casher

(Author's note: The taming strategies for all rascals have a number of things in common. Before proceeding, familiarize yourself with the strategies for change in the introduction - "Taming Your Fiscal Rascals.")

Cashers are known for their organizational skills and disciplined savings when it comes to money. In some respects, their behaviors mimic those of Asher, but they tend to be more certain about their money ideas. They are systematic savers and like to keep track of what their money is doing. Cashers tend to save impressive sums that would most likely be quite a bit larger if more diversified. Cashers, however, like predictability and are suspicious of the stock market.

Our number cruncher, Stan the Plan Man, has begun to question his savings choices lately. His interest rates have been declining every year for more than a decade. Meanwhile, he keeps reading about higher returns in mutual funds.

His wife's 401K plan was the most recent reminder of these past performances. Stan did a projection of his assets, playing "what if?" What if he had put his savings in four of the funds offered through Jan's plan? According to this calculation, he would have more than double what he currently has.

Stan scolds himself for not playing "what if?" with the numbers earlier in the game. At the same time, however, he still doesn't like the idea of putting his money in investments that could go down in value.

The Pain/Gain Ratio for Casher Stan the Plan Man

For years, Stan had gotten such a kick out of keeping a large percentage of his money in savings that he hadn't thought all that much about taking investment risk with his hard-earned dollars. He had always set aside at least 20% of his paychecks. With that amount being saved, it added up in a hurry, even without impressive growth. His money was growing with every paycheck, because he so faithfully held on to it. Stan had often heard the rule of thumb about saving 10% of pay. He thought by doing twice as much and more, he would have plenty for old age.

When he calculated the amount he needed to save for retirement assuming a 5% average rate of return and compared that to a 10% average rate, his Pain/Gain ratio began to change. Before he began calculating these comparisons, the pain of saving such a large percentage of his earnings did not feel like a problem to Stan. It was not in question. If the computer said saving 22% of his pay was necessary, then he did it.

In Stan's view, the pain score for saving so much was irrelevant. Therefore he gave it a 2 rating. The gain was extremely important, high priority, making it a 10 on Stan's rating scale. With a Pain/Gain ratio of 2/10, his pain factor (PF) was a scant .2 - no motivation to change. But these recent calculations were disturbing to Stan because the comparisons were so dramatically different. Saving a large percentage of his income wasn't all that difficult for Stan, but at the same time, to see his large accumulations be worth only half of what they might have been gave him pause.

Added to that, Jan had been complaining for some time that they were too restricted in their budget. She had started working for a financial planner and was learning about diversification. Her questioning of their allocations, coupled with her desire to free up some of their cash flow added to Stan's increasing uncertainty. Now Stan's PF changed to 1.5 because he considered the Pain/Gain ratio to be more like 6/4. Especially when he calculated twenty more years of accumulations, raising their potential average rate of return started to seem like an idea he would consider. Jan had also given Stan much to ponder when she recited the multitude of ways they could use the money. Some of the items started to sound appealing, even to Casher Stan.

Reconstructing Casher's Bundle of Beliefs

When Stan compared his original BOB with his reconstructed BOB, this is what he saw:

Casher's Bundle of Beliefs (Original BOB in extreme)	Casher's Reconstructed Beliefs (New Goals)
1. Responsible people carefully monitor all of their money flows to get it right.	1. I am responsible even if my money monitoring is imperfect.
2. I should keep all of my money in guaranteed interest accounts so it can't go down.	2. I can diversify my savings and still honor my low risk comfort zone.
3. You never know when an emergency need will arise, so savings is most important.	3. Savings and spending deserve to be balanced according to my goals.
4. If I don't track every penny, my finances are out of control.	4. My finances are in control, as long as I know generally where my money goes.
5. It is wasteful and totally foolish to buy things other than necessities.	5. It is important to enjoy some of the fun, pleasant things money can buy.
6. Taking any risk with my money means it could all go away.	6. There are many choices that could increase my return without risking all the principal.
7. Life is serious business, and it's wrong to use money for enjoyment.	7. It is good to enjoy life and allow money to sometimes be used for enjoyment.
8. I should take care of my financial management without any help.	8. It is wise to get help with my financial management, so that I broaden my understanding and choices.

Stan found his highest "presence intensity" (PI) scores in the following beliefs:

- *Responsible people carefully monitor all of their money flows to get it right.*
- *I should keep all my money in guaranteed interest accounts so it can't go down.*
- *If I don't track every penny, my finances are out of control.*

A defining moment

As we have seen with many of the previous rascals, one of the problems of a misguided belief is in an overly strict or extreme definition of a word in the statement. Three of the problem words in Stan's first belief are "responsible," "all" and "right."

Stan valued integrity and responsibility. The problem with Stan's criteria for judging whether he was behaving "responsibly" with his money was his severe, no-exceptions-allowed mentality about it. By trying to keep track of "all" his money, he had become overly strict in his watchfulness. When he missed some of the minor expenses in his cash flow, he became grumpy and irritable. His definition of "right" was also open to reassessment. Stan had previously defined "right" as having 100% accuracy in his accounting.

In all three words, Stan had been aiming for perfection. Now he thankfully questioned such a rigid standard. "I am a responsible person even if my money monitoring is imperfect," gave Stan some much needed flexibility.

The discussion of Stan's questioning his old assumptions about having all his money go into guaranteed interest accounts, was described as part of his Pain/Gain ratio. He was beginning to explore other asset allocation mixes that would still be conservative in nature, yet provide a greater potential for raising his average rate of return.

Stan, similar to Asher, sought total control of his money. It was not fraught with worry the way Asher's was, but it was similar in its objective. Stan's definition of having adequate control had evolved into an unrealistic standard. He was relieved when he was able to redefine "adequate control" as knowing generally where his money was going.

Stan found that he could use all of the reconstructed beliefs in reviewing his financial style. For example, he welcomed the belief, "It is important to enjoy some of the fun, pleasant things money can buy." Stan remarked, "Hey, that sounds familiar. That's what Jan's been saying. Maybe she's starting to rub off on me. Whatever. It feels right, even though it goes against how I used to be." Jan, at this point, could be observed attempting to contain her urge to gleefully scream out, "It's about time!"

Casher's AIM: Changing and Balancing Habits

Stan, as a Casher rascal, felt that his physical habits with money were still okay, as long as he wasn't too rigid about the frequency and extent to which he sought accurate records. He was already evaluating his savings choices and his AIM would start by moving some of his guaranteed interest accounts into funds with higher potential returns. He would move small portions to gain comfort with his new choices, and continue shifting more as his expanded comfort zone allowed.

Similar to Basher in his disallowance of fun, Stan was going to try out Acting As If Modified in his prioritization of fun expenditures in his budget. If fun was a higher priority, Stan knew, he would pursue more of it. Stan and Jan decided to plan more fun into their week.

Stan reviewed Casher's mental and emotional habits with money and rewrote all of them to fit a more balanced approach overall. He also decided to seek advice from his financial planner on how he could adjust his asset allocation and still honor his low risk preference.

He had seen that there was a risk in getting too low a rate of return and he wanted to broaden his understanding of the many other risk factors when making decisions about where to save money. Besides market risk, there were also taxes, inflation, liquidity and interest rate risks to consider. Stan felt ready to AIM at being more of an investor.

Casher Visiting Other Rascals

There was little danger that Stan would become a compulsive spender, so he visited the foreign habits of Rasher and Flasher. Like

Basher and Asher, Casher needed a little help imagining what he would have fun doing. Stan borrowed the idea of observing what others say and do from Flasher, as an intriguing research project about spending habits of "splurgers." One of the ideas that appealed to both Stan and Jan was planning a vacation with friends. From Rasher's social habits list, Stan decided he would like to be more actively involved in buying some gifts for loved ones throughout the year.

Action Honoring Awareness (Aha!) Ideas

Decrease accounting reports: Stan decided to reduce his number crunching tasks by doing his accounting once a week instead of three times a week. He would still use his accounting software, because it saved him time when preparing tax returns. What he would do less of, however, was printing all the different variations of reports that he felt duty-bound to examine in countless ways. He would start by printing two reports just once a month, and consider decreasing that frequency to quarterly reports. His spending was so controlled that his need for frequent examinations was unnecessary.

The theme of the new awareness that Stan had gained by getting acquainted with the Casher beliefs and habits was that he had simply become too narrow in his definition of acceptable practices of a responsible person. His habits were the ones that Flasher, Rasher, and Dasher, for example, needed to do *more* of, but *he* needed to start doing *less* of.

Budget unstifling: Stan had the luxury of being able to let go a bit, even blow some money now and then. He decided to honor that awareness by adding a category to his stifled budget: *"wild money."*

Loosening up: In previous years his money use had been so tame, that Stan decided he needed an opposite word to remind him that he had earned a new right. "Wild" was a word that gave Stan a little jolt, which is what he said he needed to loosen him up enough to follow through on some of these new ideas. Otherwise, he mused, his default would throw him right back into the non-spontaneous "Stan the Plan Man" tendency of building structures so concrete that they became a prison without any doors or windows. He did not want to be stuck inside that rigid structure any more.

Casher Celebrates AIM and Aha Successes

Stan had never given himself much credit for what he did get done, as he felt totally duty bound to be accurate and responsible. As we have seen, his Casher tendencies had become overly dominant and restrictive in their command over Stan.

He had unknowingly gone overboard in his quest to be financially in control. He first congratulated himself on the positive benefit that had come from his great discipline and control of money. He used this as his "bill of rights" to get acquainted with a more relaxed style. Stan kept a PAT journal and noted all the positive aspects of new habits he was practicing.

Stan gave himself permission to experiment a little and make adjustments as he went along, which helped prevent him from being trapped in any one particular new habit. When he exercised his right to use his "wild money" he reported to Jan that he had been successfully wild and wildly successful. This reinforced his broadened definition of "success" to include a little nonsense or fun now and then.

Summary of Taming Strategies for Casher

♦ Claim the old beliefs that have misguided you.
♦ Revisit them and be on the lookout for others.
♦ Reconstruct them to create new, useful beliefs.
♦ Claim and tame any sneakers that have strayed into your rascal.
♦ Begin including spontaneity as part of your plan.
♦ Look at your Pain/Gain ratios for insight and clarification.
♦ Visit other fiscal rascals for ideas and take AIM and Aha actions.
♦ Make note of your positive changes and celebrate them.
♦· Seek other professional opinions as you make adjustments in your financial plans.
♦ Build in freedom to adjust any new or old structures you have built.

Stasher

*I am a **Stasher** and I say, "Let's grow!"*
Bank interest rates are dull, that much I know!
I rarely spend, I'd much rather invest,
And make great profits -- that's what I think's best.
So I keep my eye on the changing Dow,
And catch a ride that gives me a big WOW!

Claiming Stasher

"Stashers" - crave to save in the stock market and are similar to Cashers, except they are investors who **stash** money wanting it to *grow* substantially. So, instead of squirreling it away in "safe" places, Stashers invest it with a willingness to take higher risks in order to get potentially higher rates of return.

Stasher characteristics are similar to Cashers' in the desire for control, record keeping and future security. Stashers have been known to expend considerable energy and fuss over money matters and may have to watch out for taking too much risk or refusing to enjoy some reasonable spending in the present. Stashers, like all of the rascals, have some very useful skills and traits unless they become overly dominant and out of balance. An extreme Stasher may almost get addicted to the stock market. Rather than crave to save and grow money, these extremes crave the big hit or the big win in the market in a similar way that a problem gambler gets "hooked."

Case History: Sally Rally Stasher

Meet Sally Rally Stasher. Named for her optimistic view that the stock market will always rally in her favor, Sally wasn't always quite as extreme in her securities trading as she has become today. Sally began innocently enough, with an interest in making her money grow well so that her "stashed" money would appreciate in value after inflation. In a financial planning seminar, Sally appreciated being exposed to the idea that by starting early, the growth of money could be dramatic. Sally had seen others neglect savings until rather late in life and she didn't want to make that mistake.

Sally's first exposure to the stock market was when she started an IRA. Sally looked at the long term performance figures of the mutual fund choices in the plan and became quite enthusiastic about the double digit returns of the stock funds. She made her choices by simply picking the four funds with the highest ten year average returns. Although she knew from the literature that past performance did not guarantee future results, inside she hoped to get the same returns or better. Sally became dissatisfied with her savings account because of the small interest rate and put it all in an aggressive growth mutual fund, even though she was saving for a house and hoped to have the down payment in less than two years.

After her first year in the IRA, Sally became eligible for her company's 401K plan, so she participated in it rather than her IRA. After several years in the plan, Sally had experienced periods of both growth and decline. She figured her funds had averaged a little over 10% rate of return during the time she participated in them. At first she felt satisfied. Her IRA of $2000 had more than doubled (to $4120) in seven years. Sally would hear stories, though, about stocks that had doubled in a year or less. She thought, hmmm...if my IRA had doubled every year, it would now be worth $256,000!! Her $4120 suddenly looked minuscule by comparison.

What Sally didn't think about in her excitement over the thought of doubling her money every year was the feasibility of picking the right stocks every single year for such a doubling to occur. Sally's friend at work talked about a newsletter he got that told him the top ten stocks every month. His stories sounded like winners every time and soon Sally subscribed to the newsletter. Sally began buying the stocks she read about. She read about timing systems to help her know when to sell the stocks. This built up her confidence in what the outcomes would be.

Sally began to invest larger and larger sums in her eagerness to realize big gains. The portion of her income that she invested grew and soon she had difficulty meeting ordinary expenses. She cashed in her IRA and bought stocks with it. The "trading" game was taking more and more of her time, her thoughts and her emotional energy. Her results were discouraging, however. Many of the stocks depreciated in value. Even her house money fund had gone down. Had she stuck with the "boring interest rate" she would now have accumulated enough for the down payment on a house.

When Sally's IRA value dropped to $1100 she began to question the validity of all the success stories she had been listening to. That's when she asked her friend if *all* of his stock picks had turned out as well as the success stories he shared with her. It was a question she hadn't thought to ask before. The answer? More times than not, the stock values went down and her friend never realized the gain he might have, had he known what was going to happen next. Knowing when to get out of a stock wasn't so fool proof after all. The rally Sally had counted on was not happening, yet she still felt hooked on the potential. The power in Sally's Stasher money personality, when overly dominant like this, left her with money shrinking instead of growing.

The Sally Rally Stasher Profile

As with the other fiscal rascals, we begin the Stasher profile by reviewing the BOB, the four kinds of money handling habits (PETS), and some COOL/FOOL rules that may be exhibited by Stashers. Think about how the *italicized* words impact expectations and other results.

Stasher's Invisible Bundle of Beliefs
(Original BOB in extreme)

1. The stock market is the *only* place to be.
2. If I *move* it around *a lot*, I'll probably *beat the game*.
3. There is *nothing* more enjoyable than trying to get *great gains* in the market.
4. I need the excitement of stocks for *all* of my savings.
5. The one with the most money is the most *successful*.
6. The one with the most stock market *activity* is superior.
7. I'm not satisfied until I know I have *enough* to stop working.
8. I may not be able to keep my income going, so I need to stash *most* of it.

Stasher's *Physical* Habits of Handling Money

- Actively involved, may delegate some management.
- Reads about (and may study) investing.
- Invests in stocks, stock mutual funds, or higher risk investments.
- May have a financial planner, unless perceives such a relationship as interfering.
- May get caught up in risky stock trading.
- Fairly organized about bill paying and recordkeeping.
- Utilizes "good debt" only (e.g., mortgage).
- If uses credit cards, pays off balance each month.
- May have entrepreneurial, fluctuating income.

Stasher's *Emotional* Habits With Money

- Secure, satisfied (when accumulating assets)
- Impatient (for high growth/return on investments)
- Bored (by shopping or fixed interest rate accounts)
- Competitive (in finding better and better growth on investments)
- Clever, stimulated (by high returns)
- Determined (to accumulate large sums of money)
- Disturbed, frustrated (when investments fail to perform)
- Superior (to spenders or conservative investors)
- Restless (if feels is investing too little)

Stasher's *Thought* Habits With Money

- Prefers investing over spending and has a higher risk tolerance than other rascals.
- Not interested in shopping.
- May avoid spenders or conservative savers.
- Likes knowing rate of return on investments.
- Seeks higher income careers, even if more risk involved.

Stasher's *Social* Habits With Money

- Likes activity (but may get overextended commitments).
- Flexible about entertainment choices.
- Occasionally treats others.
- Gives gifts for important events.
- Prefers menu-serviced restaurants (tips reasonably).
- May loan money if assesses it to be a good risk.

COOL/FOOL Rules Stasher Mistakenly Created

- Put *all* your savings in stocks and make *frequent* trades.
- Use your capital gains to measure your *self worth*.
- *Never* stop trying to beat the game.
- *Feel superior* to others not trading in the stock market.
- Stash a *large percentage* of your income, in case employment ends forever.

145

Taming Stasher

(Author's note: The taming strategies for all rascals have a number of things in common. Before proceeding, make sure you have reviewed the strategies for change in the introduction - "Taming Your Fiscal Rascals.")

Sally Rally Stasher, like other fiscal rascals, started out her adult life with a set of reasonable sounding financial goals. She wanted to start her savings early, rather than neglect it and lose the time value of her money's growth. Sally also knew she wanted it to be invested for growth. The dilemma Sally got into was one of seeking to fulfill her goals by continuing to do a better and better job of it. To Sally, that meant seeking higher and higher returns. After all, she wanted growth. The way to be more successful in that pursuit, she reasoned, could only mean experiencing more and more growth. If 10% was good, 15% was better, and so on.

Sally also got caught up in the excitement and the occasional reinforcement of her pursuit. Every now and then, one of the stocks she had picked was a big winner. The occasional winners kept her playing the game even though the big losers seemed to outnumber the big winners. The winners gave her the hope that this was the easy way to make money and reach her goals sooner. This seemed like a realistic pursuit when Sally got caught up in the moment, but reality did not seem to match her hopes and feelings. Nevertheless, the excitement of the winners had gotten her hooked into thinking she could win often enough to come out ahead.

When a Stasher rascal becomes overly dominant, this is what can happen. Whereas a dominant Casher saves money in pursuit of too much safety, a dominant Stasher saves money in pursuit of too much return. The problem with an extreme Stasher's "saving" by over-investing in higher and higher risk investment vehicles, is that it takes on traits that are more like spending than saving. If the investment risks all the principle, or worse (as when buying on a margin in the stock market), *money starts to go, instead of grow.* An overdone Stasher is more like our old overspending rascals Flasher and Rasher. Too much money is being sacrificed into the black hole of spending. Stasher "spends" her money on poor investments, resulting in similar problems as Flasher or Rasher. The money has gone away and the rascal is left with little or nothing to show for it.

The Pain/Gain Ratio for Sally Rally Stasher

Let's take a look at how the Pain/Gain ratio worked in Sally's case. When Sally first started "stashing" money, she was satisfied with her returns. She would say her money and the energy she expended to stash it was a low pain compared to the gain. Her ratio was 4/8, making a pain factor (PF) of .5. With a .5, why did Sally start to change? The answer lay in her change in beliefs and expectations. Her 10% returns started to seem inadequate and her perceived satisfaction of them (gain) went down as her expectation of finding higher returns went up. Now her gain rating dropped to a 2, changing her ratio to 4/2. It was this elevation in her pain factor that brought on her change into riskier investments (4/2 = 2 PF).

If Sally had contained her risky investments to a smaller proportion of her total invested money, her Pain/Gain ratio might have stabilized. But instead, Sally went overboard on the dollars she was putting at risk. She put all of her IRA money into individual stocks, when it had been earning an average return of 10%. She even used her savings account money to buy stocks. And from a cash flow standpoint, Sally was "spending" more and more of her income on risky investments. Luckily, this hadn't been a choice in her 401K plan, or Sally might have started rearranging it, too.

Sally's results were quite discouraging. Her IRA was now worth only about one fourth of what it had been, the savings account that would have helped her buy a house was depleted, and her cash flow was so tight she was feeling squeezed. The rally Sally had hoped for, wasn't happening. This created more of a drain (and pain) than Sally ever would have imagined when she started out.

All those super double digit return stories were proving impossible to consistently attain. The drain of it all was painfully elevated and the payoff was most certainly down. Sally's ratio had changed again. The pain of the risky investing became a 9 and the gain was a 3 (9/3 = 3 PF). This left Sally with a motivation to change to a less aggressive portfolio, but her confusion about *what exactly to change to,* was a big question. Sally wasn't at all sure how she would handle "giving up" on her absolute optimism about the stock market.

Reconstructing Stasher's Bundle of Beliefs

Sally reviewed Stasher's beliefs (both original BOB and restructured BOB outlined below) and found several that fit her.

Stasher's Bundle of Beliefs (Original BOB in extreme)	Stasher's Reconstructed Beliefs (New Goals)
1. The stock market is the only place to be.	1. Being only in stocks is probably out of balance and too risky.
2. If I move it around a lot, I'll probably beat the game.	2. Moving stocks around rarely beats the game.
3. There is nothing more enjoyable than trying to get great gains in the market.	3. Finding a balance of enjoyable things is important.
4. I need the excitement of stocks for all of my savings.	4. Using nothing but stocks is a risky way to find excitement.
5. The one with the most invested money is a more successful person than others.	5. Invested money is not a true measure of personal success.
6. The one with the most stock market experience is superior.	6. Stock market knowledge does not measure a person's human value.
7. I'm not satisfied until I know I have enough to stop working if I so desire.	7. I am most satisfied when I balance my work and pleasure.
8. I may not be able to keep my income going, so I need to stash most of it.	8. I can adjust and still be happy if my income or employment goes down.

Sally identified most strongly with the belief, *"The stock market is the only place to be."* Looking at this belief and searching out its mistaken part gave Sally her first insight. The word "only" implied to Sally that *all* her money should be in the stock market if it were indeed the *only* place to be. Sally could see for the first time that she had, in fact, been acting on this belief. The only money she hadn't put into individually owned stocks was in her 401K plan, and that's because the choice wasn't available in the plan.

Sally also reported a strong "presence intensity" (PI) of the belief, "I need the excitement of stocks for all of my savings." Here, Sally was claiming the problem that she had noticed developing over her active participation in the market. She had begun to feel hooked on the action and potential of a big win, almost the same way a gambler couldn't resist playing one more time.

There was evidence of people "winning big" all around her, just like in a casino. But in reality, that evidence was extremely misleading. The winners were far fewer than it appeared. They just had a way of bringing attention to themselves. What was left unnoticed were all the losses, or poor picks. Most of the players were in the hole even by the time they got in and then back out of the game.

> She had begun to feel hooked on the action and potential of a big win, almost the same way a gambler couldn't resist playing one more time.

Related to this belief was the one, "If I move it around a lot, I'll probably beat the game." Sally could see that her behavior had matched this belief. What she wanted to do now, was investigate the likelihood of beating the game. This was beginning to look like an unrealistic expectation.

Sally found the reconstructions of the beliefs helpful in bringing back a more balanced perspective. She also realized she had begun to measure her success by judging her stock market activity and this was inaccurate. Her primary new goal became one of weeding out the extremities of her problem behaviors and rebalancing her money life with her other values and goals.

Stasher's AIM: Changing and Balancing Habits

Sally looked over Stasher's physical habits of handling money and found that she had certainly gotten "caught up" in trading stocks. She could see that many of the habits had fit her before she had gotten into stock trading.

Sally decided that Stasher's habits were basically quite good, as long as she followed an asset allocation model that wasn't so lopsided. Sally had a financial planner that she had not met with in more than two years, which she decided would be her first AIM change. Her goal was to be a *balanced* Stasher (her tamed money rascal), rather than a wild, untamed fiscal rascal.

> **Sally decided that Stasher's habits were basically quite good, as long as she followed an asset allocation model that wasn't so lopsided.**

Sally decided to redo her spending plan based on what she should be saving if she were getting an average rate of return of 10%. Her financial planner would calculate the figures and meet with Sally to review different growth-oriented asset allocation models. By Acting **As If Modified** to a tamed Stasher, Sally felt she could begin rebuilding her portfolio to include some stock activity, but with a smaller overall emphasis and proportion.

Sally also realized she had become narrow in her social activities and decided to look for other ways to fight boredom when it struck. She wanted to find ways to rebalance her emotional life by gaining new experiences that would give her greater satisfaction in areas other than her narrow focus of investing and asset growth.

Stasher Visiting Other Rascals

Sally visited Casher for ideas on the conservative component of her financial plan. She also looked at taming strategies for Flasher and Rasher, as she recognized the hyper-spending component of her con stant stock trading. Sally Stasher also felt she had too little awareness of her own values, so she visited Basher. For ideas on ways to broaden activities she looked at our busy rascal, Dasher.

Action Honoring Awareness (Aha!) Ideas

Some of the specific ideas Sally was ready to take action on right away. Her awareness of the Stasher balance that she was seeking, started with changing her asset allocation on the money she was saving from her current income.

Goal-based asset allocation: Instead of using it to buy stocks, she would select four to eight growth-oriented mutual funds recommended by her financial planner. The amount she would invest monthly would come from the calculations for her retirement goals and an assumed rate of return of 10%. This way her cash flow would be more in control and would be based on her goals instead of her urge to splurge on stocks.

Less aggressive choices: Sally redefined her stock purchases as entertainment spending and would limit that to $100 per month for three months. This amount would not be considered part of her serious retirement investments. She wanted to allow for some of her "old passion" in order to get a limited dose of excitement. If she felt she was getting hooked into the old lure of hitting it big, or if she simply tired of it, she would stop her stock purchasing altogether.

Realistic expectations: Sally also was given many resources from her financial planner that showed her some studies of market timing and their actual returns. This would help her gain more realistic expectations about her own chances in stock picking. The old emotional habit had mislead her into believing she could hit it often enough to substantially improve on what the professionally managed funds could do. The actual statistics said differently.

Portfolio advice and relaxed pace: Sally would seek more professional advice on the stock portfolio she had put together. This would include the securities she purchased in her IRA and the transfers she had made in her savings account. She would make her "buy" and "hold" decisions gradually, based on the information she was getting. This way she was not moving all her money at once in a reactive move that might be as wrong as some of her earlier decisions to buy stocks in the first place.

Continuing education: As Sally reallocated these investments, she would use her new asset allocation model to honor her growth orientation. Because Sally enjoyed learning about investment strategies, she enrolled in workshops on mutual fund investments and retirement planning.

Community service: Sally also decided to volunteer once a week to work at her community food shelf. She was aware of the *values void* that her previous habits had seemed to "fertilize" and this action gave her a focus that simply made her feel good. She knew it helped her minimize her restless feeling. Part of her actions to honor awareness strategy was to look for community needs and help in ways she could, without getting overly analytical about it.

Stasher Celebrates AIM and Aha Successes

Sally maintained her PAT (Positive/Accomplishment/Thankful) journal and shared her changes with a good friend of hers who was interested in balancing her own financial habits. Her friend (Rasher) had gotten into trouble with credit card debt. Together they discussed their values and the distorted meanings that money had come to have for them. By celebrating their liberation from overspending, they felt many new feelings of simple satisfaction and contentment. They discovered they most enjoyed doing activities that were low in cost and high in social service.

Summary of Taming Strategies for Stasher

♦ Claim the old beliefs that have misguided you.
♦ Revisit them and be on the lookout for others as you go forward.
♦ Reconstruct them to create new, useful beliefs.
♦ Claim and tame any sneakers that have strayed into your rascal.
♦ Look at your Pain/Gain ratios for insight and clarification.
♦ Visit the other fiscal rascals for tips and take AIM and Aha actions.
♦ Reallocate your investments over time.
♦ Change the amount you are investing to fit specific goals.
♦ Redefine stock purchases as entertainment, and do it in minimal amounts.
♦ Record your positive progress and celebrate it.
♦ Begin defining overly aggressive investment risk as over spending.

Fiscal Rascals in Relationships

Before we married we were fine with money,
But now what I am seeing isn't funny.
The fun's not fun now that my date's my spouse,
We can't even save enough for a house!
I'm scared I might not have done the right thing,
What kind of problems might this marriage bring?
I thought we shared the same philosophy,
But what that means, we simply can't agree.

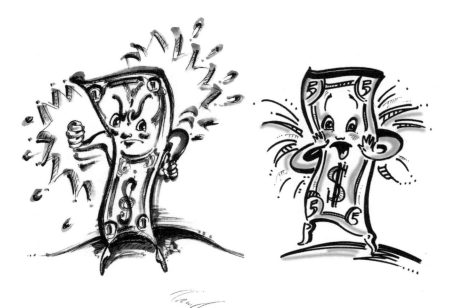

Opposites Attract AND Clash

It has often been said that opposites attract. This is frequently the case with money styles. In short, the very thing that was part of the attraction in courtship may turn into the source of irritation and clashing when money is merged.

A cautious penny-pincher may enjoy the new excitement in a relationship with a flashy spender. The engagement headlines might read: *"Flasher spices up life for Casher!"* Casher, for example, may subconsciously have the view that when it's someone else's money disappearing to extravagant outings and luxurious gifts, the courtship is exciting. It's a way for Casher to loosen up a bit, compared to the usual disciplined restrictions with money. But when they marry, it's no longer someone else's money getting eaten up, and soon Casher is way beyond the old comfort zone. The excitement wanes and turns into resentment.

> **In short, the very thing that was part of the attraction in courtship may turn into the source of irritation and clashing when money is merged.**

Certain themes occur:

- *One rascal cannot relate to where the other is coming from (but doesn't inquire or listen, either).*

- *One or both rigidly believe their way is the only way to be, and the other should change or the marriage is over.*

- *They've never discussed goals, expectations, priorities, histories or preferences with money management.*

- *One or both expect the other to "tend the tender."*

- *They discover they have different philosophies and don't know how to handle the variance.*

- *One feels superior and wants the control and power with $.*

156

If only we knew our BOB before we got married

Even when two similar rascals get together, one might emerge as the superior spender, saver, worrier, etc. This is because of a natural comparative process that occurs between two parties.

Remember the story of Kay, whose alcoholic father was known to overspend the family's money? We can make some guesses about what kind of a mate she'll find if she doesn't discover her invisible beliefs about money. Even though she didn't like her father's money behaviors, the likelihood that her spouse will exhibit those traits is high.

This is because Kay is at risk of choosing the familiar over the imagined, or wished for. Just as Kay felt somewhat uneasy in saving money because of invisible beliefs, she could feel uneasy with a partner that doesn't do what she unconsciously *expects*. Kay's invisible beliefs could easily betray her conscious desires if she is unaware of them.

Conflict Resolution Tools

Comprehensive conflict resolution and intervention is beyond the scope of the money rascals book. However, the money rap map worksheets and conflict information in the next few pages can be a helpful resource for couples. These tools can be very useful for couples who have some or most of the ingredients listed for handling conflict well (see "Recipe for Resolving Conflict" in this chapter).

If, on the other hand, these attributes are already absent in the relationship, then the intervention and assistance of a good counselor is recommended to help resolve persistent, stubborn, or intensive arguments. A marriage counselor can assist with learning to communicate in new ways, so that each member is heard and goals can then be discussed and agreed upon.

In addition, please refer to, "The Fiscal Rascals Get Married" poem on the next page for an "*arhymatherapy*" look at how the money rascals may pair up when opposites attract. Try to locate themes you can relate to, chuckle at yourselves, then use the tools to begin to resolve conflicts.

The Power in Your Money Personality

Yahoo! I'm **Flasher** and I've found a mate,
Good looking, well trained and makes me look great!
My spouse looks so good tucked inside my arm,
I get to have my way, so what's the harm?
With all our money I can spend for two,
I just don't get why that makes my mate blue.
What is the problem with a little debt?
I can't see why anyone has to fret.
As long as I'm the center of attention,
No other problems are worthy of mention!

I am an expert when it comes to shopping,
But now it's me my spouse has thoughts of dropping!
I find great sales and gadgets for us both,
Yet now I'm asked to take a savings oath.
A faithful **Rasher** couldn't dream of such,
I need my spending as my impulse crutch.
I can't imagine any other way,
Than having fun spending up all our pay.
And if my mate is not content with that,
Our marriage will be done in no time flat!

I chose a marriage partner, good for me!
So why do sometimes I just want to flee?
Being a **Clasher** is tough on a mate,
Like nibbling on some kind of rotten bait.
At first you think you're into something good,
But then "should not" changes right into "should."
Our biggest trouble is not knowing goals,
It makes it hard to have any controls.
If I am saving, then my spouse is spending,
Our inconsistency is never ending!

Exciting, yes! I'm going to get married!
What better reason to feel rushed and harried?
It is my **Dasher** way to dash about,
And not leave time for any kind of doubt.
Sometimes my mate can dash along with me,
But then wears out and will just let me be.
I hope my spouse can organize the money,
I'm much too busy - I can't be the one-ee,
I'm sure it will all work out fine and dandy,
As long as someone ELSE is fiscal handy!

Before we married we were fine with money,
But now what I am seeing isn't funny.
A **Basher** knows selflessness is the key,
And life should be lived very modestly.
I've been so careful about what I own,
Now my mate's doing things I don't condone!
I thought we shared the same philosophy,
But what that means, we simply can't agree.
I just want to make sure I'm a good soul.
And share that with a partner, that's my goal.

I'm scared I might not have done the right thing,
What kind of problems might this marriage bring?
It wasn't easy going it alone,
But now I'm in an unfamiliar zone.
Because I'm **Asher,** worry takes it's toll,
And leaves me feeling so out of control!
I wish my mate could take the fear away,
So I could actually have a fret-free day.
If only I had automatic money,
I might be able to enjoy my honey!

When we were courting my date brought such fun,
I was the practical accounting one.
Well, I'm still **Casher -** I want money safe,
But at this rate I'll be a homeless waif!
The fun's not fun now that my date's my spouse,
We can't even save enough for a house.
It's easy to save money and keep track,
So why can't my partner stay in the black?
This stranger used to like my great control,
But now I'm supposed play some other role!

I love my spouse BUT when it comes to money,
My outlook's better, for it's bright and sunny!
As a smart **Stasher** I am in the know,
I'm sure I'll make our money really grow.
When I'm accused of getting carried away,
My answer is to promise big future pay.
There's no good reason to slow down our stashing,
Not even if we take a major thrashing.
It's worth it for the riches it could bring,
In spite of a little marital sting!

When things start to look SHADY

As the poems reveal, the rascals start to cope in unhealthy ways. The acronym SHADY refers to coping behaviors that do not promote healthy money communication in relationships. **S**neak, **H**ide, **A**void, **D**eceive and **Y**ell are all indicators of conflict that most likely will escalate unless new ways of dealing with financial differences are found.

The SHADY coping tendencies put some aspect of the relationship in the dark, blocking the light - or bright side - that could exist in a healthy relationship. Deception, aggression or avoidance may bring temporary relief, but almost never result in a harmonious outcome.

At times, much of the problem is due to confusion or uncertainty about what the best steps financially are for the couple. In these cases, a financial planner is a good resource and can clarify the multitude of choices and needs.

The tools offered in this book are designed to help individuals understand themselves first, and begin to make changes to enhance financial and emotional outcomes. When both members of a couple can do this and begin to *think* about money in a new way, they can open the door to a new way of *talking* about it.

By looking at the emotions and belief systems of ourselves and our partners, we can enhance our understanding of how we have interacted in our financial lives. It can help us fend off defensive reactions and attacks on each other when we comprehend the underlying force of each other's styles with money.

When two people begin to tame their own extremes, compromises about differences are more successful. The old SHADY ways are ruled out and CHATs (**C**ommunication **H**onoring **A**mended **T**endencies) become the new norm.

Now, review the communication tools on the next few pages and give them a try!

Recipe For Resolving Conflict

Ingredients needed to enhance communication and find solutions:

Communication Style
Openness and authenticity.
Listening for understanding, not for preparing what to say next.
Both individuals are able to admit when they are wrong.
Absence of defensiveness and competition.
Recognize and affirm each other when problems are resolved.

Mutual Objectives
Desire for harmony and comfort in the relationship.
Willingness to spend the time required to resolve the issue.
Determination to deal with conflict, rather than neglect it.
Both have an attitude of give and take.
Focus on partnership winning, rather than one person or the other.
Agreement that disagreement does not mean one is right and the
    other is wrong.

Feelings
Deep *respect* for self and partner.
Enthusiasm for finding solutions.
Appreciation for uniqueness of partner.
Desire to keep relationship free of resentment.
Belief in their compatibility as a couple.

Realistic Expectations
Differences in opinions and style.
Each partner makes mistakes and is sometimes wrong.

☺☹☺☹☺☹☺☹☺☹☺☹☺

Couples have a much greater chance of resolving conflict when they
have learned how to combine the above ingredients as a way to
"keep their cool" when differences arise. If some of these are absent
in the relationship, the "Rap Map" exercises can help. Blending all the
ingredients together creates a more harmonious partnership and an
enhanced ability to make changes and compromises when needed.

Money Rap Map   PAT Chat Guidelines

Brief discussions about money will be called a "rap" or "chat." Begin and end each CHAT with a PAT (positive-appreciative-thanks) for each other. These are expressions of positive things about your partner - things you appreciate, or saying thanks for something specific to your partner. See Pre- and Post- PAT CHAT lists. Negotiations to modify behavior should only be done after CHAT themes have been confirmed and understood. You are working on eliminating useless communication patterns. That's why CHAT stands for Communication Honoring Amended Tendencies. So, no more knocking, rocking, mocking, docking, balking, gawking, and socking talking! **INSTEAD use the guidelines below as a map:**

1. Rapper (speaker): Share in advance the theme of the talk needed, and ask if the partner is willing to *listen for understanding*. Wait for a response. Accept a no as well as a yes.

[Themes = DOC: Difficult thoughts/feelings; Okay/Neutral, or Change negotiations.]

2. Listener: Answer yes only if you will listen with an open mind and will resist interrupting and anticipating responses. If you answer no, you must initiate the rap later, usually best if in the same day.

3. Rapper: Limit rap to an agreed upon time limit (clock talk 3-5 minutes), being as efficient in the message as possible. Use "I" as:

[e.g., I feel __(emotion)__ when __(action)__.]

4. Rapper: Say "I'm finished" when you have completed expressing your message.

5. Listener: Mirror or paraphrase back what you heard being expressed, then ask, "Have I understood what you intended?"

6. Rapper: Respond to mirroring with yes, no, or a restatement to clarify any part of your message that was received inaccurately.

7. Listener: Mirror message again until rapper affirms the rap was understood accurately.

Pre PAT CHAT

Money Rap Map

Choose and complete one of the following sentence stems to establish a harmonious atmosphere before you begin your money rap:

- ☺ I look forward to experiencing this in our future:
- ☺ One of the things I enjoy most about you is:
- ☺ I am still attracted by your:
- ☺ One way we make a great partnership is:
- ☺ I'm thankful for your special ability to:
- ☺ One of the ways you've helped me grow is:
- ☺ We work well together when we:
- ☺ I feel valued when you:
- ☺ I appreciate this about your money behavior:

Post PAT CHAT

After talking about each difficult issue, always recognize positive aspects of what went well, then validate with wrap-ups, such as:

- ☺ I think we made progress in discussing:
- ☺ When we can converse this way, I feel encouraged to:
- ☺ I am thankful for you sharing this with me:
- ☺ I appreciate your listening to:
- ☺ I think we should be proud for accomplishing:

Rap Encouraging Wrap-Ups

- ☺ What I'm proud of about the effort I've made today is:
- ☺ One of the things I appreciate about your effort today:
- ☺ Some of the important awareness I've gained about myself:
- ☺ I am glad that you told me ____ because now I'm aware of, and can be sensitive to:
- ☺ An idea I have to reward ourselves is:
- ☺ The main Aha! I got today was:

The Power in Your Money Personality

The people who raised me handled money

spending behaviors: saving behaviors:
conversations about it (or lack of, or fights, etc.):
allowances for all the kids:

My early recollections about money

my handling of it, feelings about it:
of family members:
of friends:
of school or church teachers:

The COOL and FOOL rules or expectations I came to have

from people I admired:
from conflicted relationships (ways not to be):

I hoped money would buy me

(choices: success, significance, social acceptance, family approval, control, joy, independence, personal value, security, love, freedom, power, respect, serenity, other meanings that seem to fit)

My money traits now

My dominant values about it:
My management style with it:
Rascal traits I like and want to keep:
Rascal traits that have caused problems:
Rascal traits I want to begin to amend:
Ways you can help me make changes:

In previous relationships (If relevant):

I was good at (or appreciated for):
We never seemed to be compatible regarding:
My main mistakes were:
I think my partner's main mistakes were:
Boundaries about my tolerances that I learned:
Fears I developed as a result that I want to heal:
There wasn't enough of (or was too much of):

Goal Clarification and Alignment

Make separate lists of goals you have for yourself individually and for your partnership together. This can include general career and income goals, housing, recreation, travel, retirement, children's education, community or church involvement, relationship goals or health goals (physical, mental or spiritual).

1. For each goal you list, rate it on a 1-10 scale for intensity of desire, with 10 being the strongest. Those you rate as 8, 9 or 10 represent ones that feel like necessities to you and do not feel optional. To give them up would seem like a sacrifice too great to bear.

The goals rated 5-7 are those you would like to accomplish, but are more optional. It would be disappointing if they were not met, but not devastating.

Finally, the goals you rated 1-4 are the "nice to haves." These are more like wishes that you could give up rather easily, but if things go well, you would know what to grab next!

2. Add the age by which you want to achieve the goal (write as A60, for example).

3. Indicate an estimated cost by the goals that require the most money. If you don't know the cost, but believe it will be significant, write a "$____?" next to the goal. Put a heart, or any other symbol you like next to the goals that feel good but won't cost money.

4. Share your goals with your partner, and be sure to abide by the money rap map. First, decide on two joint goals from each of your lists that you agree are high priority partnership goals.

Now, choose two individual goals from each list upon which you both agree.

Do either of the joint goals conflict with any of the individual goals? Will time frames need to be adjusted? For example, if you both want to take a nice vacation every year, but you both agree you want to retire early, how will that be remedied? Is there uncertainty about cost or what is needed to accomplish the goal if it is long term? If so, use advisors to help you determine costs and methods to increase the likelihood of reaching the goal. (For example, a travel agent can help you predict travel costs, but probably couldn't help much with what you need to be saving now for retirement income in 25 years. A financial planner can help you with that, as can specialized financial calculators, books, software, or financial planning seminars.)

Merge the remainder of your lists, prioritizing as a couple and discussing any conflicts that arise. Adjust the desire scores or time frames if you discover that you have too much to achieve in too little time.

You may find you like your partner's ideas better than your own. Adjust and be happy with this discovery! If there are items you can't agree on yet, decide not to decide, and research instead. Or there may be goals that can only be accomplished if your household incomes can be raised. If that isn't feasible, put them on "temporary cancel." That means you aren't necessarily giving up, but the way to get it done is not yet a reality.

Congratulate each other on the goals that are aligned and discuss steps you will take to make sure they happen.

Fiscal Rascal Concepts

I'm getting ready to take a new look,
At all the concepts that were in this book.
And when I have a little look around,
I find my money beliefs do abound.
I'll change my habits from the inside out,
That's what my tamed rascal is all about!

Review

Now that you have read case stories and examples for each rascal, let's review some of the concepts that have been presented.

Belief Ghost Busters

Your feelings are a measure of whether a belief is lurking (like a ghost) beneath the surface of your reactions. At first, the information may be murky and difficult to see. The reason it is important to get in touch with this, is that positive change will be limited or impossible if you deny the existence of belief systems. Remember, just because some beliefs are invisible doesn't mean they aren't there! The trick is to find them and remove their distortions. Think of it as belief ghost busting!

Carbon monoxide is another way of picturing invisible belief systems. It is invisible, tasteless and odorless, but if your exposure to it is prolonged, it can kill you! Although your invisible beliefs can't literally kill you, they can do extensive damage because of their tremendous influence on the decisions and choices you make.

Your emotions are like a belief detector. Just as seeing a running car in a closed garage or a buzzing carbon monoxide detector should indicate to you that carbon monoxide is present, a strong emotional reaction should indicate that a belief is present (or a bundle of them). It is important to determine what the beliefs are, so that you can begin to make a conscious effort to eliminate the ones that are useless or damaging your potential for wise financial decision making.

How to Discover Your Belief Systems

As we have seen in case examples, our own belief systems may be invisible to us, yet influencing the direction we move in. By discovering what they have been, we can identify new directions for our lives.

The money rascals have acquainted us with several possible bundles of beliefs (BOB) in each type. If you want to identify additional BOBs relative to money or any other issues, such as marriage or careers, you can "test" yourself.

When testing for invisible beliefs, ask yourself:

"What kinds of things would I do if I believed _____ ?

By filling in the blank with a belief, you can then begin to brainstorm the kinds of behaviors you might expect to see. If you want to try it without feeling threatened, plug in a belief from a rascal that you think characterizes someone other than yourself. Perhaps you are frugal and disciplined about your spending. Then go to the Flasher or Rasher rascal.

Let's use one of the beliefs from Flasher (the prestige seeker) as an example:

"Buying the most expensive things makes me worthwhile."

To brainstorm the types of behaviors we would guess might be exhibited because of the belief, plug it into the above question:

What kinds of things would I do if I believed: _____
(buying the most expensive things makes me worthwhile?)

Assuming you wanted to feel valued and worthwhile, your brainstorming list of behaviors would probably include:

- *Buying expensive things frequently.*

- *Displaying the expensive things (because you are letting others define whether you are worthwhile or not, so why bother if they don't see it?).*

- *Buying expensive gifts for others (another way to "announce" to them that you are worthwhile).*

- *Avoiding the purchase of inexpensive things.*

- *Being judgmental about whether others are worthwhile based on whether their things are expensive or not.*

The Power in Your Money Personality

This brief list illustrates the way the belief *aims* a person in certain directions. The beliefs steer us *toward* certain habitual behaviors and *away* from others.

This concept can be used in reverse to flush out why we aim ourselves in a direction we don't understand. Like Kay, we think we are trying to accomplish a goal we are aware of, but our own choices end up sabotaging that goal.

What we can ask ourselves in reverse is:

What belief is lurking in me and aiming me in this other direction?

At times what we discover is troubling, yet when we test it out by asking what kinds of things we would be doing if we believed it, our past actions reveal it is a match. This is how some people first get in touch with self-esteem problems.

Beliefs may be discovered such as:

I don't deserve: *(a good job, a loving mate, wealth, etc.)...*

I'm no good at: *(math, planning, saving, earning, .etc.)...*

In the first discovery, the individual would most likely report that he/she wanted a good job and a loving mate. But the actions would assure that neither would happen, at least, not for long. The good job would feel too much like a mismatch, and the individual would feel terribly uncomfortable because the underlying belief doesn't fit. The next thing you know, action is taken to assure loss of the job. The same thing happens with life partners. A loving mate to a person who feels undeserving, will not be a lasting thing. The "undeserving" person either starts picking fights (which upsets the loving feeling), runs away, or chooses an unloving person to prove the belief.

In the second example, if the individual believes, "I'm no good at. . ." what behavior will be avoided? The answer is the very behavior that's

170

filled in the blank. The problem is that often the belief is distorted or untrue. One of the first things to do is to challenge the accuracy of the belief. One needn't be a math whiz to be **good enough** at it. *It is as though the actions are chosen to provide proof that the misguided belief is true.*

The easiest way to modify a belief is to remove the negative. Until the first example is changed. . .

> **from:** *"I don't deserve"* . . . **to:** *"I do deserve. . ."*

. . . there is little likelihood of receiving or retaining the "undeserved" thing. To turn that around and have a better chance of receiving and retaining it, use the "would do" question to begin discovering new habits of behavior that can lead to new results:

> "*What kinds of things* **would I do** *if I believed* **I deserve a good job**?"

This question can generate a list of things that you would do, as well as things you would not do. These activities lead to the taming concepts for each fiscal rascal called **AIM** (Act **A**s **I**f **M**odified) and Aha! (**A**ction **H**onoring **A**wareness). The action steps are the best way to reinforce changed beliefs, and get improved results.

Same action, different meaning

You may have also noticed that in some cases, the same practices were recommended for rascals that are the opposites. Although the practice is the same, the benefit for that particular rascal is quite different. A financial plan to Cashers, for example, gives them "permission" to spend money, whereas to Rashers, it shows them why overspending needs to be curtailed. The plan reveals the same information to each, but provides them with a different meaning.

Another practice recommended for any rascal, is to set aside a regular time to pay bills and attend to other money management activities, including thinking, analyzing, or goal setting. This serves as a preventative to over-planning for Casher, a preventative to over-worrying for Asher, and a preventative of negligence, or under-planning for Dasher.

A financial plan puts goals in perspective

Although the primary purpose of the fiscal rascals is to gain insight into the psychological factors of money habits, it is important to recognize the reinforcement of your effort that a financial plan can create. A comprehensive plan captures and quantifies your goals and helps you think about your priorities both long term and short term. It shows what kind of savings you would need in order to have enough income when you stop working. Without quantifying goals using the analytical calculations, it is impossible to know if you are on track with spending or saving.

No matter what your dominant fiscal or money rascals are, a financial plan can create perspective in many money matters. Without it, a significant piece of the puzzle is missing, and so is genuine peace of mind.

Remember your sneakers

Changing habits is not an easy task. Remember, stray beliefs can sneak into your psyche at any time, especially during stressful periods. All it may take is just one "sneaker" to trigger an old habitual belief or coping behavior that gets you going again on a misguided track. One reader aptly compared it to her effort in trying to rid her lawn of crab grass. She thought she had covered every possible area of her lawn that might sprout the problematic grass. But all it took was one missed section or a single seed to cause the crab grass to take over her lawn again. Stray beliefs, if missed, can take over our actions, especially when they are more familiar to us than the "new and improved" ones.

Reviewing the Pain/Gain Concept

Understanding what your payoff, or gain, has been from certain behaviors can serve you well in many of life's challenges. It can assist greatly in your effort to change.

Let's use Pat's story (from the introduction) as an example to review the Pain/Gain concept. When Pat made a big income, it was actually draining and painful to him because he felt guilty and disloyal. When Pat was initially asked on a 1-10 scale of how painful this was, he gave it a pain rating of 8. Then when asked to rate the resulting gain he felt when he made a large income, Pat gave it a 6. He said he enjoyed the money, but not as much as he expected. Pat's Pain/Gain ratio, then, on this one item was 8/6, which gave him a pain factor for earning high income of 1.3. When the PF is greater than one, change is likely.

That explains why Pat began changing his selling behavior. His discomfort with the guilt feelings exceeded his joy of achieving his income goals, so he had artificially and unknowingly "fixed it." Pat had mistakenly concluded that he had to make his income go away in order to make his uncomfortable feelings go away. His unproductive selling behavior fooled him into believing he was still working hard (a family value), yet removed what he unconsciously believed to be the source of the problem (money). In reviewing his values and other goals, however, Pat wanted a fitting solution.

Pat had sought consultation because of his problem with inconsistent work behaviors and feeling uncomfortable with large earnings. His identified goal was to achieve his sales goals (creating large income) by being consistent in his productive behaviors.

In fiscal therapy, Pat discovered that many of the beliefs underlying his painful feelings were mistaken. He decided to choose not to believe the belief! Now that the invisibility had been removed, he could see what needed reconstruction in the problem beliefs. Pat rejected the belief, "Rich people are unloving and uncaring, so if I am rich I will lose being loving and caring."

In his reconstruction of that belief alone, Pat was able to separate loving and caring from financial earnings. He also could dispel the fear that he would lose the love and respect of his family members. These beliefs were Pat's financial baggage and he was glad to lose it.

In working through the distorted aspect of his beliefs, Pat's pain rating changed. Now his ratio was 3/6, so his PF had *decreased* from 1.3 to a .5. Now Pat's gain exceeded the pain, so he had a better chance of resuming and this time, maintaining the consistent work behaviors he had identified as desirable.

Pat still had some discomfort with high earnings, but that was primarily due to his inexperience with it, rather than painful feelings of guilt and fear. Notice Pat's perception of gain about earning the income hadn't changed. He still enjoyed earning a good income, but it was not affected by changing his beliefs about what the money meant.

By maintaining awareness of what our actions have cost us verses what their payoff has been, we can understand the role motivations have played in our problems. If we perceive the payoff still outweighs the cost, we are unlikely to change. Only when the cost, or pain, outweighs the gain, will we increase the probability that our effort to change a problematic habit will have lasting effect. This takes brutal honesty and much perseverance.

No Absolutes

One of the important concepts to keep in mind when studying money issues is that there are virtually no absolute rights or wrongs about it. It is all completely relative. To many of us, that is precisely the dilemma. We are left having to think about it for ourselves when, in a way, we wish someone else could or *would* just tell us what to do. We are stumped by many questions:

- *Do we save a certain percentage of our income and spend the rest?*

- *How do we know what the right percentage is?*

- *Where do we invest it?*

- *How closely must we monitor it?*

- *What if one spouse earns twice as much as the other - does that mean that one can spend twice as much?*

- *Do we merge our money or keep it separate?*

- *Help! What are the rules?*

It is difficult to think of any statement (or rule to abide by) about money that would have absolutely no exceptions.

Look at some rules of thumb that seem absolute at first glance

1. Live within your *means*.
2. Avoid *bad* debt.
3. Save *enough* money.
4. Spend *wisely*.

The italicized words are those that could have hundreds of different definitions depending on who you ask. Many would view the basic definition of "living within your means" to mean, "Spend no more than you earn." But others would challenge that, citing credit cards and other forms of borrowing as the modern way to expand their means. They would argue that it is within their means if a credit card extends them the privilege of buying now but paying later (with interest, of course).

Still others would come up with many possible exceptions to this seemingly simple rule, such as, "But what if I need to buy something that will advance my career or double my earning potential?" To some this would be a sensible exception if the probabilities of actually receiving the income increase were high. Others wouldn't even think to evaluate probabilities. Their automatic position would be, "Just go for it." To still others, this would not be an acceptable exception to the rule. Period. And what if a medical treatment is needed? Suddenly living within your means is impossible if the treatment is provided. Surely, that's an acceptable exception, isn't it?

Look at the other statements. People have different impressions and knowledge of what bad debt is. The interpretations of what it means vary. And why should we avoid it? Who says? How much savings is enough? Based on what? Why would I have so little faith as to think I have to save for the future? Am I sinning if I don't have faith that God will provide? And what is wise in the discussion of spending? Is it wise to buy a third home if I can afford it? What about charitable giving? Is it wise to purchase the perfect birthday card for my father, when he died eight months ago?

The point of this discussion is to reveal how quickly a fairly sensible sounding rule can get blown out of the water. The ultra planners of the world would argue that people should prepare for their financial emergencies. That makes sense. However, quantifying what that means in specific dollar amounts will result in multiple opinions.

175

That's because the subject is subjective

The ultra faithful would argue that the need will be filled by a higher power. And there are thousands of variations in between that all come down to the fact that money decisions are subjective, even when using very objective methods to make decisions in the first place. The rules are opinions. The opinions arise out of unique life experience (which everyone possesses), education and information gathered, and individual values and goals.

This question of absolutes cannot be ignored when attempting to provide guidelines to people in their own search for solving the money mysteries all around them. The concepts explored in *The Power in Your Money Personality* continually bump up to this dilemma. What works as a solution for one person, could aggravate the problem for another. That is why guidance is offered with caution, advising clarification of personal goals, priorities, and values. A critical step is to become aware of beliefs that need to be reconstructed to align with one's reality.

Why bother with your Bundles of Beliefs (BOB)?

The first objective in hunting down deeply held, yet previously invisible beliefs is to discover which ones have been *mistaken* and have caused harm to yourself or others. Seeing the connection between the distorted beliefs and misguided actions clarifies the origin of the problem. Reconstructing the beliefs then helps identify alternative behaviors that can be acted on.

These exercises are the only way to test whether the values and goals we think we have, are based on an accurate sense of ourselves. It is in this exploration of previously unexplored territory in our money lives that the most satisfying and lasting solutions will appear.

Keep in mind that "adjustments to the adjustments" can be made as you work on finding new habits that bring balance to your financial world. Without this important action step, the insight may be fascinating, but nothing really changes.

Many of the fiscal rascals discovered their habits had simply become too extreme and all-or-nothing in their practice. The good news in these cases is that several of the habits did not have to be completely eliminated, but instead could be modified. For example, Casher needed to pay bills and do accounting functions *less* often, whereas Dasher needed to do it *more* often.

Taming gets the rascal out from behind the wheel

Flushing out the mischievous "rascal" characteristics in our "fiscal" life helps with the maddening absence of absolutes in the financial choices we face. It can create a more reliable internal mechanism to help in making our financial decisions. This way we can prevent repeated problems and feel satisfied at the same time.

It is important to emphasize that taming doesn't totally *erase* our dominant rascal styles. Think of it as taking control of the wheel and putting our money rascals in the passenger seat. Our habits are deeply ingrained and will always tug at us to some extent. It isn't realistic to think we can boot them out of our vehicle entirely, but we *can* regain control of the steering.

By making conscious changes in our thinking and behavioral habits, it puts us back in control of the direction we are moving in. A strong dominance of Casher, for example, will struggle a bit more than a Stasher when a mutual fund account is down in value. What taming does is expand the previous comfort zone to include some new strategies that wouldn't have been possible otherwise.

We have seen the primary purpose in taming an out of control fiscal rascal is to simply *regain control and add balance.* Sometimes this involves new learning about money that we simply had never been exposed to before. By overcoming distorted beliefs that have misguided our rascal traits, a gentle taming can begin without maiming the traits worthy of preservation.

When our fiscal lives are in balance, we gain a new sense of freedom. In balance, we honor our highest priority goals and values, instead of simply giving in to our urges. The result is a feeling of greater security and financial confidence for the remainder of our lives.

Parting Thoughts of Encouragement

Getting acquainted with the money rascals has hopefully brought you new awareness of the connection between thoughts, feelings and actions. Perhaps it hadn't occurred to you before that emotions and thoughts might simply be habits. One of the objectives of the fiscal rascals has been to reveal the link between our thoughts and our own reactions and experience of life.

If we are in the habit of thinking that we are capable of handling the life tasks before us, we will tackle them with confidence and security. If, on the other hand, we are in the habit of thinking we are not capable of handling a task (such as money management), we will feel insecure or discouraged and will be reluctant to tackle the task.

Like Dasher, we may have filled our lives with other activities that effectively prevent us from attending to our money tasks. Or our efforts may be inconsistent like Clasher, or we've been in the habit of worrying and fretting like Asher.

The encouraging thought I would like to conclude with is that once we have recognized the power of connecting our thoughts with our actions and emotions, we can more easily flow into increasingly positive, healthy thoughts without having to identify all of the specific mistaken ones. We need only be aware that our negative or painful reaction is an indicator of a distorted thought. Let us now use one last arhymatherapy poem to view the tamed rascals with a rhythmic flair.

The Money Rascals Go Shopping

'Twas the time to go shopping and all through the mall,
Not an item escaped me, though my cash funds were small.
The credit cards were stuffed in my wallet with care
In the hopes I'd find something just loaded with flair.

The signs triggered my urge with "Buy one get one FREE!"
And I wanted to spend, though I knew I should flee!
My plastic will cure this, I think as I reach
For my credit card - I can buy lots of each!

"But you don't need this," sneaks in an unwanted thought,
And your money is gone from the past stuff you bought."
I DESERVE this I silently pout to myself,
And who cares if I never build any wealth?

This feels good NOW and my gosh I've been stressed,
If I don't give in, I'll end up depressed!
When what, to my tormented mind should appear,
But the eight money rascals who once caught my ear.

On Dasher! On Basher! On Casher and Stasher!
Now Clasher! Now Flasher! Now Asher and Rasher!
To the end of the debt, to control of my bills,
I'm going to conquer these darn money ills!

I've made up my mind and can adjust my aim,
I'll balance my rascals and make them all tame!
I'll be more like Casher and cut out some frills,
Turn the mountains of debt into shrinking hills!

Like Stasher, I'll make sure to save and invest
So when I'm old I can afford some fun AND rest.
And when emergencies hit I will not be pressed,
'Cuz I've got cash for that - it's the egg in my nest!

When the Flasher or Rasher impulse hits me,
I'll find a different behavior that's FREE...
Like the library, which won't take my credit card,
But they'll loan books with no bills that bombard.

In spite of my Dasher, I'll make time for a plan,
So that in my future I don't live in a van!
My plan will guide me on what spending's enough
And I won't judge my value by all of my stuff!

There will always be Jones's I can't keep up with,
Using THAT as my measure is just purely myth.
Instead, I'll treasure what matters most to me,
Relationships, balance, and health is the key.
Sorry credit cards, now you won't win the plea,
I've said good bye to clashing, hello harmony!

What an Aha! looks like

As you can sense from the journey made by the tamed rascals in the poem, it is liberating to take back the power you have in your money personality. We think a tamed money rascal might look very much like the ostrich below - relieved, excited, and free from the bondage of old, distorted or useless habits of thinking and acting.

We have the power to construct thoughts that are positive and healthy in their orientation. This significantly enhances our ability to find solutions that align with our goals and values. The result is a significantly improved financial picture and greater peace of mind.

You are in the driver's seat with all of your money rascals, and as you make changes to improve your relationship with money, do continue to validate your strengths and talents by keeping track of your progress. We all need a PAT on the back from time to time. Now you can give yourself one as often as you *think!*

Thank you for taking the time to get acquainted with the power in your money personality via the eight money rascals. Congratulations on your effort to create greater balance in your financial life by claiming and taming the characteristics that apply to you. As you go forward with your new **A**wareness, remember to **H**onor it with **A**ction (Aha!).

Whether your natural style leans more toward the **urge to splurge** or the **craving for saving**, your new actions will soon be as comfortable and familiar as the old ones once were. But the best part is that, like the tamed rascal in the poem, you will likely discover a wealth of more fulfilling and balanced results.

APPENDICES

Fiscal Rascals Assessment Questionnaire

Name _____/_____ Date _____

Circle the item that most closely fits how you are in your current life, given the situation presented. Try to pick just the one answer that is most like you, but if two have equal dominance, both can be chosen and included in your scores.:

1. My view on saving money is:
   a. It's best to regularly be earning interest in a safe place.
   b. It's most important to get good growth on it.
   c. It's impossible now because it prevents me from paying for the things I have now.
   d. Any extra should go for a good cause, like a charity or the food shelf.
   e. I can save for a while, as long as it buys me something exciting a little later on.

2. When I shop, I tend to:
   a. Look for bargains on anything, then stock up.
   b. Buy only brand names because they look impressive.
   c. Have a hard time deciding whether I deserve the item or not.
   d. Have a list of specific items I need and stick to it.
   e. Look at the Goodwill or Salvation Army stores first.

3. My financial goals are:
   a. To accumulate, invest and grow substantial dollars, especially long term.
   b. To live for today and enjoy the money I have.
   c. To try not to worry so much about money.
   d. To earn a lot and buy first class items all the way.
   e. To save a large portion of my income so that my future is secure.

4. If I won $50,000 right now, my first reaction would be:
   a. ALRIGHT!! Now I can buy something huge! Let's see, new car? house? or wardrobe?
   b. This is going STRAIGHT to the bank and it's going to stay there!
   c. Wow, in XYZ stock fund at 12%, this should double five times in six years--that's $1.6 million!
   d. I wonder what time the mall opens today!
   e. Oh, my gosh, there's no way I can manage this correctly!

5. If someone asked to borrow money from me:
a. I would be afraid I would need it later and wouldn't get it back.
b. I would feel flattered that they thought of me, and would probably lend it.
c. I'd probably do it if I had it, but it would be a hassle to keep track of!
d. I would do it if the person was a good risk and paid it back at a fair rate of return.
e. It would have to be for a worthy cause.

6. When I balance my bank statements and check book:
a. I think of it as dull and difficult.
b. I feel stressed and worry about possible errors.
c. I'm too busy to do that, but I try to keep track of the balance.
d. I've noticed I spend too much some months, yet I'm ok in others.
e. I reconcile it regularly and it's quite accurate.

7. When I have extra money, I:
a. Celebrate and treat myself or my friends.
b. Have trouble figuring out whether to spend it or save it.
c. Wonder how that happened!
d. Don't really notice or do anything differently.
e. Figure I should hang on to it in case some problem comes up.

8. My philosophy about money is:
a. Having too much might create greed or selfishness.
b. I should save enough to have a secure future, but I keep spending my savings.
c. I'm too preoccupied with other things to have a money philosophy.
d. Saving and accumulating money is more important than spending it.
e. Spend it now--you can't take it with you!

9. I use credit cards:
a. Frequently to buy items that keep up my successful appearance.
b. Rarely, if at all. It's better to put my money in a safe bank savings account.
c. Never! It's too likely that spending would get out of control.
d. For convenience only--I keep track of my budget and pay it off each month.
e. Off and on, depending on the mood I'm in.

10. The way I manage unexpected or irregular expenses is:

a. I have a savings account that I set aside budgeted money into for this.

b. I keep meaning to start a savings account for this, but I run out of time.

c. Sometimes I have it in savings, other times I have to borrow to cover it.

d. Get disgusted, then juggle my other bills to pay the unexpected ones.

e. Feel upset and worried, even if I have the money to cover it.

11. If I have debt from borrowing money:

a. I feel guilty and afraid I won't be able to pay it back.

b. I live modestly so that I never have to borrow money.

c. I sometimes forget to factor it into my expenses for paying it back.

d. It is practical and I track it with my cash flow to leverage my investments.

e. I look for the best rates and then pay it back as quickly as possible.

12 Keeping track of my spending:

a. Is no big deal because I spend so little and keep my lifestyle very simple.

b. Is impossible--it goes out faster than it comes in.

c. Is important because that's what allows me to continue my investing.

d. Is not for me--I'd rather just buy the things that look great and not sweat it.

e. Is what helps me keep my savings account growing and compounding interest.

13. When I hear the word wealth, I:

a. Feel frustrated and wonder if I'll ever have it, because my savings never seem to last.

b. Get turned off thinking of the greed it breeds and I avoid it.

c. Think of big houses, fancy cars and clothes and all the other goodies it buys.

d. Want it so that I can buy whatever suits my fancy, whenever the mood hits.

e. Worry about how it would be managed, but wonder if it would help me stop worrying!.

14. If I see something I would like to have but can't afford:
   a. I buy it almost no matter what.
   b. I tell myself it isn't necessary and I don't buy it.
   c. I think about my investments and what the real long term cost would be.
   d. If it boosts my successful image, it's worth it.
   e. I might buy it if I can figure out where I'll get the money.

15. If there is a flaw with my retirement savings, it's that:
   a. I'm under-informed about it because I haven't had time to pay much attention to it.
   b. It's modest, but should provide for my necessities, which is all I want.
   c. I started it, but then stopped saving or took some out.
   d. I keep meaning to get started, but something always seems to come up.
   e. I may be overly focused on adding to it and getting good growth on the funds.

16. What I like most about my style with money is:
   a. I enjoy buying things that make me look good.
   b. I'm too busy to think about that!
   c. I don't need or want much, so I can live simply and avoid money's evils.
   d. I'm organized and controlled about my savings and spending.
   e. Nothing. Money stresses me out no matter what's going on.

ANSWER SHEET/KEY FOR MONEY RASCALS

Now that you have completed the questionnaire, use the key below to determine which combination of funny money characters you may tend to be:

Use the columns below to score your answers (you may want to circle the character letters for each item below). Then total how many of each type you are and record them at the bottom. The one that occurs the most is the one that represents your predominant character, but it's useful to look at all of them to see how they compare to each other.

A = Asher; B = Basher; C = Casher; D = Dasher; R = Rasher; S = Stasher; cL = Clasher

Ques	a	b	c	d	e		a	b	c	d	e
1.	C	S	R	B	F	9.	F	C	A	S	cL
2.	R	F	cL	C	B	10.	C	D	cL	R	A
3.	S	R	A	F	C	11.	A	B	D	S	C
4.	F	C	S	R	A	12.	B	R	S	F	C
5.	A	F	D	S	B	13.	cL	B	F	R	A
6.	D	A	D	cL	C	14.	R	B	S	F	cL
7.	R	cL	D	D	A	15.	D	B	cL	cL	S
8.	B	cL	D	S	R	16.	F	D	B	C	A

ADD TOTALS, THEN PLOT ON CONTINUUM:

A/Asher _2_   B/Basher _6_   C/Casher _5_   D/Dasher _1_
F/Flasher _7_   R/Rasher _0_   S/Stasher _4_   cL/CLasher _1_

Urge to SPLURGE					Crave to SAVE		
Flasher	Rasher	Clasher	Dasher	Basher	Asher	Casher	Stasher
prestige spender	impulsive shopper	conflicting desires	busy avoider	money is bad	fearful worries	safe saver hates debt	growth investor

186

Appendix: Assessment Graph

	FLASHER	RASHER	CLASHER	DASHER	BASHER	ASHER	CASHER	STASHER
15								
14								
13								
12								
11								
10								
9								
8								
7								
6								
5								
4								
3								
2								
1								
Totals								

Meet the FISCAL RASCALS™ -
Those mischievous characters inside us who may be triggering our urge to splurge or craving for saving!

"Flashers" - love *flashy* purchases and depend on them to create a feeling and look of success. They are the most opposite of Stashers. Both think big - but Flashers are the image spenders. Flashers can be impulsive whose weakness, for example, may be luxury cars or name-brand clothes - items that Flashers believe create social success. Flashers may use money for power, and may feel inferior or unsuccessful without these external displays to prove their worth. Flashers sometimes may appear snobbish or competitive to the other rascals, showing off or doing one-up moves which may cause negative reactions in others. The spending also may not match with Flasher's ability to afford it.

"Rashers" - are almost the opposite of Cashers, because the last thing they want to do is "squirrel away" money! Known for making *rash* and impulsive decisions with money, Rashers' spending is like the Energizer bunny - it keeps going and going and going...! Rashers love to spend money generously and frequently on themselves and/or others whether they can afford it or not. They may be in debt because of this love. Rashers dislike (or hate) saving, budgeting, planning and tracking expenses. In the unusual event that Rashers do save any money, it's usually kept liquid so that it can be retrieved for spending desires that may arise. Goal setting and interest in the future is low priority to Rashers.

"Clashers" - are known for sabotaging their own savings efforts, because one desire *clashes* with another equally strong one. Clashers are like a "recovering" spender. They decide to get their spending under control, but every time they save up a sum of money, they end up spending all or most of it when an urge to splurge overcomes them. Clashers may have had parents with two opposing styles. By swinging back and forth between the two extremes, Clashers have difficulty finding and sticking with a healthy balance. No matter what Clashers do, they feel like they're being disloyal to one side. Clashers have a nickname, "Hasher" because decisions about saving and spending may get postponed in order to "hash over" what to do. This, of course, is impossible because the two conflicting styles don't know how to resolve their conflict. This procrastination may go on for many years or even a lifetime.

"Dashers" - *dash* around, always rushing from one activity to another--all except money activities, that is! Dashers aren't so consumed with the thrill of spending, but instead simply don't get around to planning and organizing their money. This may be due to a feeling of disinterest, boredom, incompetence, or confusion about it. Dashers may not even balance the check book or know what income is in-coming! Dashers have one thing in common with

Clashers - they may avoid money activities and procrastinate in the belief that they will "hash over" what to do - but they manage to be too busy to get to it!

"Bashers" - *bash* wealth, and may be critical or suspicious of people who like money and the luxuries it can provide, believing it may "breed greed", evil or selfishness. Bashers also may fear being criticized for having money, so they make sure to be virtuous by living a very modest lifestyle. Bashers are the opposite of Flashers, and attempt to display their virtue by rejecting luxuries. Bashers tend to earn a smaller income and may feel guilty if they keep or earn too much. Bashers may give money away or find other ways of making it disappear if they start to feel there's too much. Bashers are uneasy talking about money. They don't want to think of making profits, so may be uncomfortable investing it for growth.

"Ashers" - are burned out, *ashen* and pale in color from worrying so much about money. Ashers feel helpless and fear many aspects of money management including earning enough of it to feel secure. Ashers may be skeptical of any growth at all, and therefore, keep cash "hidden" in places like the cookie jar or under the mattress rather than trust a financial institution or advisor with it.   Usually Ashers are reluctant to spend and may be married to a spender, which feeds their fear. Ashers are the most fearful and discontent of the characters and if neglectful, it is out of anxiety over what to do with money.

"Cashers" - are the characters who likes to "squirrel away" *cash* money and keep it safe for the future. Cashers are serious goal-setting savers who like to keep track of their money, prioritize it, control it, budget it, and perhaps do just about anything but spend it! Money is security to Cashers. Cashers fear risk with money, so prefer conservative, cautious, slow and steady accumulation.   Cashers may have trouble trusting others with money and difficulty spending it on pleasure or nice items.

"Stashers" - are similar to Cashers, except they are investors who *stash* money wanting it to GROW substantially. Instead of squirreling it away in "safe" places, it's invested with a willingness to take higher risks in order to get potentially higher rates of return. They are similar to Cashers in their desire for control, record keeping and future security. Stashers may expend much energy over money matters and may have to watch out for taking too much risk or neglecting to enjoy the present.

Bills Ledger for MONTH of:

Descrip-tion/Notes	$ Amount due	Date due	$ Amount paid	Date sent	$ Balance

Glossary

Aha - Acronym for **A**ction **H**onoring **A**wareness, an encouragement concept to remind us that changes need to occur in more than just intellectual insight. Our behavior, or actions, need to be modified to be in harmony with our genuine beliefs.

AIM - Acronym for Act **A**s **I**f **M**odified, a strategy for practicing new behaviors that we have identified as an objective. AIM also used as reminder that our beliefs aim, or steer our actions in a certain direction.

Asher - The fiscal rascal who is *ashen* and pale from worrying about money issues.

Basher - The fiscal rascal known for *bashing* wealth, viewing it as sinful, greedy, or selfish.

BOB - Acronym for **B**undle **O**f **B**eliefs, which describes how we formulate interpretations of our experiences which are often distorted or inaccurate. Those that are created in childhood tend to remain out of our conscious awareness, yet they continue to steer our behavior.

Casher - The fiscal rascal characterized by a desire for accurate recordkeeping and safe savings, keeping most of it in *cash*.

Claim - Accepting the existence of our money rascal traits, beliefs, or habits.

Clasher - The fiscal rascal who has *clashing* objectives, causing inconsistent behaviors with money.

COOL - Acronym for **C**ulture **O**f **O**rigin **L**essons, represents the rules of behavior we have established for ourselves, interpreted from societal messages we may have received directly or indirectly, consciously or unconsciously.

Dasher - The fiscal rascal who *dashes* from one activity to the next, but neglects money management activities.

Appendix: Glossary

Delightful/Frightful - the concept that every money personality has positive aspects (delightful), as well as problematic (frightful) aspects. The objective is to create balance, so that the frightful traits do not dominate and cause problems.

Drain - The process of energy depletion brought on by stressful problems, represents the cost or consequence of our behavior, see also pain.

Fiscal - Any issues relating to finances or money.

Fiscal Rascal - The mischievous financial characteristics that may "visit our psyches" and influence our money behaviors, especially during times of stress.

Flasher - The fiscal rascal who seeks status or prestige through *flashy*, expensive expenditures.

FOOL - Acronym for **F**amily **O**f **O**rigin **L**essons, represents the rules, or expectations of behavior we have created for ourselves, interpreted from family messages we may have received directly or indirectly.

Gain - The payoff, or benefit we derive from our behavior. Only when the Drain begins to outweigh the Gain in our perception, are we motivated to make permanent changes.

Invisible vows - Unconscious promises we make to ourselves due to distorted conclusions reached from life experiences, especially in childhood. Although invisible, they exist and are influential in our choices.

Mistaken beliefs - Alfred Adler's terminology for thought patterns that are outside of one's conscious awareness. They are formulated in early childhood from misinterpreted data. They tend to encompass extremes such as all-or-nothing thinking and perfectionism.

Money Rascal - A tamed fiscal rascal, in control, yet still present.

Pain Factor (PF) - Used to determine motivation for change when using the Drain/Gain ratio. Divide Drain score by Gain score to get PF. When PF is greater than one, change is more likely.

Glossary, continued

Pain/Gain Ratio - A scoring system to determine an individual's motivation to change. When the pain score is more than the gain score, motivation to change is higher.

PAT - Acronym for **P**ositive/**A**ccomplishment/**T**hankful, a reminder to journal your accomplishments, things you are thankful for, or positive benefits of changes you are making. It's your "PAT on the back" for implementing new habits with money.

PETS - Acronym to remember the four components of personality: Physical; Emotional; Thoughts; Social

Personality - All the physical, emotional, thought, and social characteristics of an individual.

Presence Intensity (PI) - A rating system to identify the degree to which a trait exists within your money personality.

Questionnaire - Assessment tool using multiple choice response format to determine which fiscal rascals are one's dominant money personalities.

Rascal - Mischievous character.

Rasher - The fiscal rascal known for making *rash* and impulsive money decisions.

Reconstruct - The rewriting of mistaken beliefs to correct distortions of thinking patterns.

Sneakers - Stray thoughts that usually aren't associated with a certain fiscal rascal, but exist in our unique BOB (Bundle of Beliefs) and may sabotage our positive efforts.

Stasher - The fiscal rascal who loves to *stash* money in investments that will provide highest returns.

Tame - Subduing traits of a rascal that have caused problems in our fiscal life.

References/Bibliography

Bae, M.K., Hanna, S., & Lindamood, S. (1993). *Patterns of overspending in U.S. households.* Financial Counseling and Planning, 11-30.

Boundy, D., & Washton, A. (1990). *Willpower's Not Enough.* Harper Perrennial.

Belsky, G. (2001, September-October). *Drowning in debt.* My Generation, 64-66.

Burns, D.D. (1980). *Feeling Good.* Penguin Books.

Cash, G. (1998). *Spend Yourself Rich.* Financial Literacy Center.

Cordell, D. (1995, November). *Personal responsibility for retirement planning.* Journal of the American Society of CLU & ChFC, 58-64.

DePass, D., & Halvorsen, D. (1997, January 24). *Who is to blame for rise in personal bankruptcy?* Minneapolis Star Tribune, pp. A1, A19.

Dinkmeyer, D.C. (1988). *Adlerian Counseling and Psychotherapy.* Macmillan Publishing Company.

Dominguez, J, Robin, V. (1993). *Your Money or Your Life.* Penguin Books.

Felton-Collins, V. (1990). *Couples and Money.* Bantam Books.

Gurney, K. (1988). *Your Money Personality.* New York: Doubleday.

Hanna, S., Montalto, C.P., Yuh, Y. (1998). *Are Americans prepared for retirement?* Financial Counseling and Planning, 1-12.

Hansell, S. (1996, August 25). *Personal bankruptcies surge as economy hums.* The New York Times, pp. 1, 38.

Jeffers, S. (1987). *Feel the Fear and Do It Anyway.* Ballantine Books.

Appendix: References/Bibliography

Martinez, G.R. (1997). *Money and Me.* TreeHouse Press.

Matthews, A.M. (1991). *If I Think About Money So Much, Why Can't I Figure it Out?* Summit Books.

Mellan, O. (1994). *Money Harmony;* (1995) *Overcoming Overspending.* Walker Publishing Company, Inc.

Mitchard, J. (1997, January 4). *Credit cards - a plastic slide to disaster.* Minneapolis Star Tribune, p. E1.

Nelton, S. (1986). *In Love & In Business.* John Wiley & Sons, Inc.

Pilzer, P.Z. (1997). *God Wants You to be Rich.* Simon & Schuster, Inc.

Rutledge, A. (1994, Spring). *Are you a compulsive spender.* Money Counselor, 8, 1-3.

Seabury, D. (1937). *The Art of Selfishness.* Pocket Books.

Singletary, M. (1996, September 18). *A new breed of debtor shocks credit card issuers.* The Washington Post, pp. F1, F8.

Stern, L. (1995, February 13). *Credit-card crunch.* Newsweek, 54.

Twerski, A. (1990). *Addictive Thinking: Understanding Self-Deception.* Harper and Row.

ORDERING INFORMATION

*To order additional Money Rascal materials:
books, tapes, assessments, or for information about
workshops, training, or keynote speeches:*

Call (800) 525-5301
or (952) 432-4666

Write:

Fiscal Therapy Communications
14530 Pennock Avenue
Apple Valley, MN 55124

email: susan@zimmermanfinancial.com

WEB: www.moneyrascals.com

FAX: (952) 432-6705

ORDERING INFORMATION

Ways to order:

CALL (800) 525-5301; local (952) 432-4666.

FAX to (952) 432-6705,

EMAIL: Susan@Zimmermanfinancial.com

**MAIL to: Fiscal Therapy Communications
14530 Pennock Avenue
Apple Valley, MN 55124**

Visit our website @ www.zimmermanfinancial.com

Money Rascal Materials

book _____ quantity @ $14.95 = TOTAL $_____
audio tapes _____ quantity @ $59.95 = TOTAL $_____
workbook _____ quantity @ $ 9.95 = TOTAL $_____
shipping & handling add $4 first item = TOTAL $_____
$1 each additional shipped item = TOTAL $_____
GRAND TOTAL $_____

Thank you!

ABOUT THE AUTHOR

Susan Zimmerman is a Chartered Financial Consultant (ChFC) and a Licensed Marriage and Family Therapist (LMFT) with a Master of Arts Degree in counseling and psychotherapy. Susan specializes in blending the psychodynamics of money with financial planning. She is a noted speaker, author, and workshop leader. Susan has also created audio tapes, educational software, and other instructional materials on the subject of stress and transition management.

Susan co-founded Zimmerman Financial Group with her husband, Steve, in 1988. The mission of their registered investment advisory firm is to build and preserve their clients' net worth and help them feel confident and in control of their financial world as they move through each stage of life. Susan's light-hearted approach to money personalities helps people feel liberated to talk about finances in a new way. The insights gained and action ideas offered with the eight money rascal personalities help people make and maintain positive changes in their financial lives.